AI AGENTERPRISE: BUILDING BIG WITH SMALL RESOURCES

DEMYSTIFYING AI FOR STARTUPS

SRINIVAS MAHANKALI

Salute to the Dreamers

To the bold dreamers, the relentless builders, and the quiet warriors of change—

AI Agenterprise: Building Big with Small Resources, is dedicated to the millions of startup founders around the world who have dared to walk away from the comfort of cushy jobs, stable careers, and societal expectations to chase a vision only they could see. You've chosen the harder path—not for personal glory, but to solve real, deep-rooted problems with innovative, impactful solutions. In doing so, you've embraced uncertainty, sacrificed short-term gains, and committed yourself to the long arc of change—for the betterment of humanity.

In a world where sky-high office rents, inflated capital costs, and oversized salary expectations have crushed countless dreams before they could take flight, this book is a manifesto of hope. It shows how startups can be built smarter, leaner, and stronger—using the power of open-source technology, AI agents, LLMs, and the boundless potential of the Metaverse. It's a blueprint for turning limited resources into limitless impact.

Let this book be your companion in the storm, your compass in chaos, and your source of fuel when the world says, "it can't be done."

With gratitude and reverence, this book is also dedicated to the global visionaries—

Sam Altman, Elon Musk, Mark Zuckerberg, Satya Nadella, Sundar Pichai, Jensen Huang, and Aravind Srinivas who continue to light the way for a new generation of innovators, showing us that with imagination, technology, and courage, we can truly build the impossible.

Contents

Foreword — *vii*

Preface — *ix*

Acknowledgements — *xiii*

Prologue — *xv*

1. The New Age Of Entrepreneurs Powered By AI Agents — 1

2. The New Age Startup - Built By Code, Not Cash — 11

Global Leading New Age Startups: A Few Case Studies

3. Building A Startup With Open Source Everything — 31

4. Training Your AI Army — Agents That Work For You — 41

5. Enter The Metaverse — Work, Meet, And Sell In 3D — 55

Free Open Source LLMs And Metaverse Tools

6. Data-Driven Decision Making With AI & Analytics — 75

Integrating Technologies For Modern Healthcare

7. Scaling Through Innovation And AI-Driven Product Development — 97

8. Automating Operations With AI — 105

Digitalisation Of Manufacturing

9. Growing Your Startup With AI-Driven Marketing And Sales — 119

Contents

10. Scaling Operations With AI And Automation   132

11. Building A Data-Driven Culture For Long-Term   140
Success

12. Creating Tech-Enabled Business Models And   148
Monetization Strategies

13. Unlocking Startup Potential With The Metaverse 159
And Digital Twins

14. Building And Leading A High-Impact Tech-   166
Driven Team

15. Building AI-first Human Led Start-ups   173

16. Scaling Sustainably — Building A Profitable,   180
Impactful Business

Sustainable Scaling Guide: Profitable, Impactful Growth For Startups

17. Future Horizons — Tech Trends That Will Shape 197
Tomorrow's Startups

18. Managing Rapid Innovation   205

19. The Founder's Manifesto — A Call To Action   208

Free AI & Tech enablement tools for Founders   213

Open-source AI Agents and LLMs comparison   217

Glossary of AI, Agent, and Metaverse Terms   221

Your First 90-Day Plan with Tech Stack   225

FAQs on topic addressed in the Book   229

Foreword

A Call from the Future

By a Startup Mentor, Technologist & Futurist

As someone who has spent the last two decades mentoring founders, building companies, and closely following the ever-evolving landscape of global innovation, I've seen one truth repeat itself over and over again: startups don't fail because of lack of ideas—they fail because of a lack of access—to resources, to the right tools, and often, to belief.

But something extraordinary is happening. A quiet revolution. One that isn't led by capital-rich giants, but by scrappy, mission-driven founders armed with open-source tech, AI agents, and an unstoppable will to build a better world.

This book—AI Agenterprise: Building Big with Small Resources—is a timely and vital contribution to that revolution.

In a world where expensive office space, inflated salaries, and bloated marketing budgets can sink an idea before it ever sees daylight, this book offers a new playbook. A playbook for the bold. It maps how to harness cutting-edge technologies like Large Language Models (LLMs), open-source AI frameworks, agentic tools, and even the immersive potential of the Metaverse—not as buzzwords, but as battle-tested tools for real growth, resilience, and impact.

The future will not be built in ivory towers or billion-dollar boardrooms. It will be built in tiny apartments, co-working spaces, garages, dorm rooms, and digital back offices—by founders like you, guided by books like this.

Read this with an open mind and a brave heart. Your startup journey might just change forever.

Yourr AI Companion!!

Preface

Before We Begin: My Journey, Your Spark

To the Founder in the Making:

Every startup begins with a dream. But dreams alone don't build companies—grit, strategy, and smart execution do.

The idea for this book **AI Agenterprise: Building Big with Small Resources**, was born out of hundreds of conversations with founders who had brilliant ideas but limited means. Startups that deserved to scale, but didn't, because they didn't have the luxury of deep pockets. I watched as inflated costs and overcomplicated systems crushed potential before it could take shape.

But I also saw something else: a new wave of possibility. A shift.

Today, thanks to the explosion of open-source technology, cloud-based platforms, and AI-powered agents, the barriers that once kept innovation out of reach have crumbled. Startups now have access to the same firepower once reserved for tech giants—if they know where to look, and how to wield it.

AI Agenterprise: Building Big with Small Resources to empower Startups is a blueprint for this new era.

Startups are no longer defined by size or budget. They are defined by speed, precision, and leverage. The digital age has ushered in a new era where small teams with powerful tools can outperform entire departments of the past. At the center of this revolution is agentic AI—an evolution of artificial intelligence that mimics not just human output, but human agency.

As I immersed myself in the journeys of today's most agile and ambitious startups, one truth became abundantly clear: agentic AI is no longer a futuristic luxury—it's a foundational necessity. The new breed of startups are no longer merely digital; they are becoming autonomous, decision-capable organisms powered by context-aware intelligence that mirrors human intuition. This book captures that evolution.

Startups like Darktrace and Aisera are at the forefront of this shift, embedding adaptive AI agents that don't just follow programmed instructions—they learn, evolve, and act independently, making real-time decisions to protect systems or serve customers proactively. This move from rule-based automation to true autonomy is revolutionizing how startups think about scale and execution.

Agentic AI isn't generic—it's deeply vertical. Companies like Hippocratic AI in healthcare, Enhans in retail, and Penciled in personalized learning tailor these intelligent agents to solve high-stakes, industry-specific problems. These aren't one-size-fits-all bots—they are precision-built solutions tuned to the frequency of their domain's needs.

Then there are platforms like Beam AI and CrewAI, which give startups the scaffolding to scale intelligently. These frameworks allow businesses to embed AI agents into their existing operations seamlessly, customizing behavior while ensuring compatibility with their enterprise DNA. The ability to scale rapidly without overhauling existing infrastructure is, perhaps, one of the most underappreciated superpowers of agentic AI.

But let us not forget: true innovation doesn't replace humans—it elevates them. Startups like Moveworks and

Adept AI exemplify the beauty of human-AI collaboration, where agents handle the repetitive, the analytical, and the immediate—while humans focus on empathy, creativity, and judgment. This harmony ensures that automation amplifies humanity, rather than eclipsing it.

The results? Dramatic gains in cost efficiency and productivity. Consider Hippocratic AI's virtual nurse agents, which deliver critical care support at $9/hour, compared to the $60+/hour industry average—without compromising on quality or compassion. Such shifts unlock scalability for startups that once found it hard to compete against incumbents.

This preface is not just a curtain-raiser—it's an invitation. An invitation to understand that startups of tomorrow are being forged not just in incubators, but in algorithms. They are not just driven by hustle and hope, but by systems of intelligence that think, act, and grow with them.

As you journey through this book, keep one idea in mind: The AI agent is not your replacement; it is your multiplier. Use it wisely—and build boldly.

Inside, you'll find not just theory, but action—tools, platforms, frameworks, and proven practices. You'll discover how to build with less, launch faster, and grow sustainably—without compromising your vision. This is a field guide for rebels, hackers, and architects of the future.

My hope is that this book ignites something in you—a spark of belief, a strategy to scale, and the realization that even the smallest startup can change the world.

Because in the end, it's not about building the next unicorn.

It's about building what matters.

Srinivas Mahankali

https://autokrater.com (Your Agentic AI Companion)

Acknowledgements

Powered by Many

This book AI Agenterprise: Building Big with Small Resources, would not have been possible without the unwavering support and encouragement of the people around me.

To my family—your patience, love, and belief in my work have been the foundation of everything I do. Your support gave me the freedom to explore, experiment, and evolve without fear.

To my colleagues, mentors, and team members—thank you for challenging me, inspiring me, and walking alongside me on this ever-evolving journey through technology and entrepreneurship. Each conversation, debate, and brainstorming session has helped shape the thoughts in this book.

A special note of appreciation goes to the digital educators who work tirelessly every day to democratize learning. Platforms like YouTube, Udemy, Coursera, and many others have been instrumental in nurturing a culture of self-learning. To the countless mentors and creators who publish up-to-date content, often for free or at minimal cost, you are the unsung heroes of this revolution.

To the search engines and AI companions—Google, Bing, Perplexity, and ChatGPT—thank you for being my research partners, ideation buddies, and tireless assistants, always ready to answer a question or spark a new thought.

And finally, to the innovative tools and platforms—HubSpot, Notion, GitHub, and many others mentioned in this book—thank you for empowering startups to build smarter, scale faster, and dream bigger.

This book is a small tribute to all of you—builders of the future, enablers of change, and champions of possibility.

With deepest gratitude,
Srinivas Mahankali

Prologue

The Tipping Point

The rain beat hard against the cracked glass window of the co-working space.

It was 10:37 PM. Everyone had left. The office boy had turned off most of the lights, but the soft glow of a dying laptop screen still lingered in the farthest corner of the room—where he sat, staring blankly at his pitch deck.

Another rejection. Another investor who wanted "traction first." Another month closer to running out of savings.

He had once held a high-paying job at a global tech company. An enviable role. Corporate travel. Monthly bonuses. But something inside had always nagged at him—what if I could build something that actually solved a real problem? Something with impact. Purpose. Something he could call his own.

So, like thousands of other dreamers, he jumped.

No fancy office. No VC warm-up calls. Just grit, coffee, and a laptop.

But what they don't tell you about the founder journey is this: it's not the sleepless nights that hurt most. It's the loneliness. The weight of choosing purpose over paycheck. The silent judgment of friends. The guilt of not contributing to the household like before. The relentless whisper: Maybe you were wrong.

That night, though, something changed.

While browsing for alternate tools to keep his startup afloat, he stumbled upon a rabbit hole—open-source LLMs, no-code platforms, AI agents, Metaverse collaboration apps, and community-driven resources built not by corporate giants, but by people just like him. A new world was opening up. One where capability wasn't constrained by capital.

He wasn't alone. Thousands—millions—were navigating the same storm. Some failing. Some pivoting. Some quietly winning.

And it hit him—What if someone wrote a guide for founders like me? One that wasn't about billion-dollar valuations, but about building with what you have? About creating sustainable impact using the best tools of our time, with the least resources?

That question became this book.

AI Agenterprise: Building Big with Small Resources to empower Startups, is more than a guide—
It's a movement.
A mindset.
A call to the brave hearts building quietly, without headlines or hype.
This book is dedicated to those who left comfort behind to chase a vision.
To those who believe technology should serve humanity—not just shareholders.
And to every founder who still believes that with the right mindset and tools,
A small team with a big dream can change the world.

CHAPTER ONE

The New Age of Entrepreneurs powered by AI Agents

"Every startup begins with a dream. But not every dream survives the storm."

The startup journey has always been a balance of vision and resilience. While entrepreneurship is often romanticized — with tales of overnight success and breakthrough innovations — the reality is far more complex. Many startups don't fail because the idea lacked merit; they fail because execution is hard, survival is harder, and scaling requires more than grit.

But a monumental shift is underway. We are entering an era where the startup game is being rewritten — by intelligent systems, AI agents, decentralized tools, and immersive technologies. This new age of entrepreneurship allows a solo founder or a lean team to build, operate, and scale like never before. The barriers between vision and execution are collapsing — fast.

This chapter explores two key dimensions: the timeless truths about startup survival and the transformational impact of AI agents in reshaping what it means to be an entrepreneur in 2025 and beyond.

1. The Startup Struggle: Unfiltered Realities of the Early Journey

Despite the hype, most startups face brutal headwinds. Not because of bad ideas — but because of blind spots, poor execution, or structural oversights. Let's explore the most common pitfalls that derail early-stage ventures.

a. Falling in Love with the Product, Not the Problem

Many startups obsess over tech, not traction. They build feature-rich platforms without validating if users even want them.

Example: A SaaS startup built a year-long roadmap for AI-powered HR dashboards — without checking if HR teams had the time or need to use them.

Lesson: Fall in love with the problem, not your product. Use design thinking. Talk to 50+ real users before writing a single line of code.

b. Underestimating the Go-To-Market (GTM) Strategy

Product without distribution is just potential energy. Founders often neglect marketing, sales, and partnerships — the real engines of growth.

Example: A fintech app won design awards but lacked a GTM plan. Six months after launch, it had only 500 users — mostly friends.

Lesson: GTM is not an afterthought — it's oxygen. Validate acquisition channels early. Build your distribution muscle in parallel with your product.

c. Burning Too Fast, Too Soon

Startups often squander early funding on superficial wins — premium offices, overhiring, or inflated marketing — before validating fundamentals.

Example: A mobility startup burned 40% of its $2M seed round on brand campaigns before understanding core unit economics. It shut down within 18 months.

Lesson: Operate lean. Obsess over CAC, LTV, burn, and runway like your survival depends on it — because it does.

2. The Resource Conundrum: Time, Talent & Trust

In startup life, everything feels scarce — but the most limited resources aren't always money.

a. Time is Your Scarcest Currency

Founders juggle too much. Not all effort drives impact.

Reality: 80% of outcomes come from 20% of effort. Prioritize ruthlessly.

Action Tip: Use OKRs or the Eisenhower Matrix weekly. Block deep work hours. Say no more than you say yes.

b. Talent is Critical — and Retention is Tough

Your first 5–10 hires can make or break you. You're hiring partners, not just employees.

Example: An edtech startup hired ex-corporate leaders who left due to chaos. Morale and momentum both crashed.

Solution: Hire missionaries, not mercenaries. Prioritize passion, adaptability, and ownership over resumes.

c. Trust is the Glue That Holds It All Together

Ego clashes and role confusion destroy fragile teams.

Fix: Over-communicate. Set cultural non-negotiables. Do retrospectives. Create a feedback-rich environment.

3. The Global Opportunity Shift

Survival may be local, but growth is now global. Remote-first teams, global product-market fit, and access to international capital are changing the startup game.

a. Remote-First, Borderless Execution

You can build a global team from day one — across time zones, with no physical HQ.

Example: A bootstrapped SaaS firm scaled to 10,000 users with a distributed team in 7 countries.

Toolkits: Slack, Notion, Deel, Remote.com, and async collaboration norms are the new operating system for modern startups.

b. Global Product-Market Fit

Localization unlocks new markets. What fails in one region might thrive in another.

Example: An Indian healthtech tool found strong traction in Southeast Asia — due to demographic similarities and growing digital health push.

Approach: Run lean international tests. Launch pilots, landing pages, or test ads before expanding.

c. Access to Global Capital & Communities

Founders today don't need to rely on local VCs. Global accelerators and investor networks are just a pitch away.

Resources: YC, Techstars, Sequoia Spark, Antler, and OnDeck all support international startups.

Tip: Build in public. Share traction, insights, and updates on LinkedIn and Twitter — it attracts smart money and smart people.

4. The Tech Disruption Trinity: AI + Agents + Metaverse

What electricity was to the industrial era, AI agents are to today's digital economy. We're witnessing the rise of autonomous entrepreneurship — where systems powered by artificial intelligence don't just automate, they think, decide, act, and evolve.

AI agents are flipping the traditional SaaS (Software as a Service) model into what we now call Service-as-Software

(SaaS 2.0 or S²S). This emerging paradigm signifies a major shift in how value is delivered through software. Here's a breakdown of the concept and its relevance across industries:

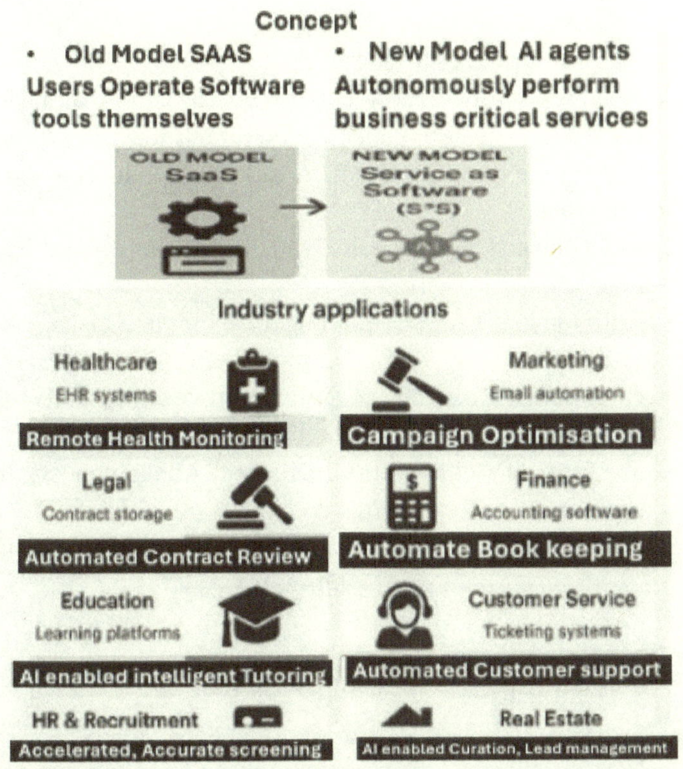

AI Agents: Service as a Software - The New Model

What Is "Service as a Software"?

Traditionally, SaaS platforms provided tools for users to perform tasks—email marketing, CRM, project management, etc. However, users had to operate the tools manually.

With AI agents, software performs the service itself. Instead of users logging in to do the work, the agent autonomously executes tasks—engaging leads, writing content, scheduling meetings, optimizing campaigns, analyzing legal contracts, and more.

Analogy:

SaaS: You rent a car and drive it.

Service-as-Software: A self-driving car shows up, takes you where you need to go, and even refuels itself.

Service as a Software: The new model in the data driven world

Key Characteristics of the New Model:

- Autonomous Execution: AI agents complete tasks end-to-end.
- Continuous Learning: Agents improve with time via data feedback loops.
- Multi-Agent Collaboration: Different AI agents work in sync like departments in a company.
- Personalized & Proactive: Services adapt to each user in real-time without needing prompts.

Applications Across Industries:

1. Healthcare

Old SaaS: EHR systems, appointment schedulers.

New Service-as-Software: AI agents monitor patient vitals, alert doctors, schedule follow-ups, and handle insurance billing autonomously.

Example: Remote health monitoring bots, AI scribes for doctors, auto-diagnosis support.

2. Legal

Old SaaS: Contract storage, case management tools.

New Model: AI agents review legal documents, summarize contracts, flag risks, and draft agreements.

Example: DoNotPay AI legal assistant, Luminance contract review bots.

3. Marketing

Old SaaS: Email automation tools, analytics dashboards.

New Model: AI agents create, test, and optimize campaigns across channels. They reply to leads, write content, and track results in real time.

Example: Agentic systems like FlygBit where content is auto-generated, optimized, and distributed.

4. Finance

Old SaaS: Accounting software, budgeting dashboards.

New Model: AI agents automate bookkeeping, detect fraud, file taxes, and recommend investment strategies.

Example: Autonomous financial advisors, AI-powered accounting bots.

5. Education

Old SaaS: LMS (Learning Management Systems) and video conferencing tools.

New Model: AI tutors personalize lesson plans, grade assignments, and adapt based on learner behavior.

Example: Khanmigo by Khan Academy, intelligent tutors in apps like ScribeSense.

6. Customer Service

Old SaaS: Ticketing systems and chat platforms.

New Model: AI agents understand customer issues, resolve them in real-time, and escalate only when needed.

Example: GPT-powered service agents, AI call centers.

7. HR & Recruitment

Old SaaS: Job posting and applicant tracking tools.

New Model: AI agents scan resumes, conduct initial interviews, evaluate candidates, and onboard new hires.

Example: Paradox Olivia, AI recruiter bots.

8. Real Estate

Old SaaS: Listing platforms, CRM tools.

New Model: AI agents automatically find properties, engage buyers, schedule visits, and suggest pricing strategies.

Example: Zillow + GPT agents for auto property matching and interaction.

<u>**Why It Matters Now:**</u>

- Drastic Cost Reduction: Fewer human hours needed.
- Scalability: Agents work 24/7 without fatigue.
- Mass Personalization: Agents can adapt per user.
- Accessibility: Even small businesses can now access "virtual staff."

Welcome to the new era:

- A solo founder can launch a global SaaS business in weeks with AI copilots.
- A 5-person team can scale like a 50-person org using agents for marketing, sales, and support.
- A startup can operate and engage customers entirely in a virtual world — no physical space required.
- This is no longer sci-fi. It's startup reality in 2025.

From Dream to Execution — at Lightspeed

With tools like GPT-4, CrewAI, LangChain, and Spatial.io:

- Product specs are written by ChatGPT.
- UI is designed by AI-driven design tools.
- Customer support runs 24/7 via intelligent agents.

- Founders pitch investors in 3D virtual rooms.
- Community-led governance is powered by smart contracts.
- Startups that embrace this shift will outperform — and outlast — those that don't.

5. The Founder of the Future

In this new age, the most successful founders won't just be hustlers or coders — they'll be architects of intelligent systems. They'll think like strategists, build like technologists, and lead like systems designers.

To thrive, they must embrace:

- AI Agents for execution at scale
- Low-code tools for rapid prototyping
- Spatial platforms for immersive engagement
- Ethical frameworks for building trust at scale

Your competitive advantage is no longer your team size —

it's your ability to leverage intelligence (human + artificial).

Are You Ready to Build in This New Age?

This chapter sets the stage for a deeper dive into the building blocks of AI-powered entrepreneurship:

- **How the Tech Disruption Trinity is reshaping startup models**
- **What AI agents mean for team structure and productivity**
- **How to launch, scale, and differentiate with immersive tech**

- **What mindset and skillsets founders need to stay relevant**

The dream is still alive — but the way to survive and thrive has changed. The question is no longer can you build it? The question is — can you build smart, fast, and sustainably with AI at your side? Let's find out.

CHAPTER TWO

The New Age Startup - Built by Code, Not Cash

"In the past, launching a startup meant chasing capital before chasing customers. Entrepreneurs spent months — sometimes years — pitching investors, building teams, renting office space, and burning through funding just to get a product off the ground. Success was often measured by how much you raised, not how much value you created."

But the startup playbook has fundamentally changed.

Today, you can start a tech company from your kitchen table using nothing but a laptop, open-source software, AI copilots, and global digital infrastructure — often without spending a rupee.

? *How the Game Has Changed*

? The Old Playbook

- **Raise Money** — Pitch VCs before you build.
- **Hire People** — Build a team before traction.
- **Build Product** — Spend months creating an MVP.
- **Sell & Scale** — Burn money on ads and sales teams.

This model was expensive, risky, and dependent on gatekeepers.

?? The New Playbook

- *Validate with AI* — Use tools like ChatGPT, Claude, or Mistral to ideate, test assumptions, and simulate customer interviews.
- *Build with Open Source* — Leverage GitHub projects, no-code platforms like Bubble, and low-code tools like FlutterFlow to spin up MVPs in days.
- *Replace Teams with AI Agents* — Use CrewAI, LangChain agents, or Autogen to simulate product managers, marketers, designers, and support reps.
- *Sell via Automation* — Launch digital funnels with tools like Zapier, Make.com, or Meta ads; onboard users with AI-driven support bots.
- *Scale via Feedback Loops* — Use data analytics tools (Mixpanel, Amplitude) and real-time feedback to improve rapidly. Tap into global freelance/remote ecosystems.

This new model is faster, leaner, and infinitely more scalable — without capital dependency.

? Why Now Is the Best Time in History to Build

- We are at a convergence point of technology democratization. Here's why building a startup today is easier, cheaper, and faster than ever:
- Free/Open LLMs: Tools like Mistral, LLaMA 3, and OpenChat rival GPT-4 in performance — and cost nothing.
- No-Code/Low-Code Tools: Platforms like Glide, Thunkable, and Appgyver enable app building without writing a single line of code.
- Virtual Offices: The Metaverse and spatial platforms like Gather.town or Spatial.io let distributed teams work together in immersive environments — no rent required.
- AI-Powered Automation: Autonomous agents now manage support tickets, write emails, handle lead gen, and even update websites in real time.
- Global Freelance Marketplaces: Access to top talent on Toptal, Upwork, and Fiverr means you can scale without full-time hires — and work across time zones seamlessly.

? Real-World Examples of "Code-Not-Cash" Startups

- Solo SaaS Founders: Entrepreneurs using GPT-4 + CrewAI to design, code, and launch products solo — managing everything from UX to onboarding with AI copilots.
- $10k MRR Solopreneurs: Creators building newsletter automation tools, niche AI bots, and digital courses that bring in predictable revenue — with zero employees.
- Open-Source-First Startups: Teams that gain user traction with free, community-led tools (e.g., LangChain, AutoGPT), and then raise capital after

proving PMF — not before.

Key Elements You Need (And They're All Free)

Need	Tool	Use
MVP Development	Appsmith, Budibase	Build app visually
Website	Framer, Astro, Hugo	Free hosting too
Project Mgmt	Taiga, Plane	Agile boards, issue tracking
Marketing	MailerLite, Canva	Email + design
AI Agents	LangChain, CrewAI	Automate tasks
LLMs	Ollama + Mistral	Local language model
Metaverse Office	Spatial, Mozilla Hubs	Remote work in 3D
Programming Help	GitHub Copilot (Free for students), Codeium	AI pair programmer

Table 2.1 Free Tools to Power an Enterprise Buildup

? Key Insight: The Barriers Have Collapsed

- You don't need a team.
- You don't need capital.
- You don't even need to code anymore.

What you need is clarity of thought, strategic leverage, and a willingness to adapt faster than legacy companies or old-school founders.

Startups are no longer built on capital—they're built on capability.
Not on how much you spend, but how smartly you build.

In this age, intelligence (both artificial and human) is the new currency.

The founder of the future doesn't just raise money — they raise systems, scale through code, and succeed by design.

A Founder's Reality

In the startup world of the past, each role in a company was worn by a different person — a CTO to code, a CMO to market, a CFO to manage finances, a sales team to close deals, and a designer to craft the user experience. Founders were primarily visionaries or managers, overseeing the orchestra from the conductor's podium.

That's no longer true.

Today's founder is the orchestra.

Thanks to AI, automation, and global digital infrastructure, modern founders wear multiple hats without burning out:

- **The Coder** – Using tools like GitHub Copilot or Replit AI to write and debug production-level code.
- **The Marketer** – Using Jasper, Copy.ai, or ChatGPT to create social media content, landing pages, email campaigns, and growth experiments.
- **The Investor** – Managing financial projections, burn rates, and even raising capital through AI-prepared pitch decks and virtual due diligence platforms.
- **The Product Designer** – Using Figma + AI design tools to create beautiful UIs with drag-and-drop simplicity.
- **The Sales Team** – Automating outreach with tools like Apollo, Lemlist, or Instantly, and closing deals with AI-generated demos and chatbots.
- **The Analyst** – Monitoring performance using dashboards built in Notion, Google Looker, or DataDog.

And yet...

They still sleep 8 hours a night.

Why?

Because AI handles 60% (or more) of the execution — freeing founders to focus on vision, decisions, and high-leverage actions.

? Mindset Shift: From Scarcity to Leverage

The biggest transformation isn't technical — it's mental.

Old Mindset:

- "I need funding to build."
- "I need a team to start."
- "I can't do this alone."

New Mindset:

- "I have everything I need — if I know how to use it."

Welcome to the Leverage Era.

In this new game, the winners aren't the ones with the most capital — but those with the highest leverage.

? **Leverage = Tools × Knowledge × Community**

- Tools: Free and low-cost software that acts as your team — AI agents, no-code builders, automation bots.
- Knowledge: Know-how on what to build, how to market, and how to grow — accelerated by books, communities, and mentorship.
- Community: Other founders, builders, and creators who help you validate, promote, co-build, and even sell — your digital tribe.

This book is your blueprint to mastering all three.

It's not just about surviving in the new startup world. It's about thriving with the least friction, maximum velocity, and zero permission needed.

Global leading New age startups: A few case studies

In this chapter, let s look at 15 startups leveraging *agentic AI* and *automation* across various domains, with examples of how they apply these technologies to drive innovation and efficiency.

Agentic AI refers to AI systems capable of autonomous decision-making, planning, and executing complex tasks with minimal human intervention, often integrating advanced reasoning, natural language processing (NLP), and automation. These startups are transforming their respective industries by harnessing these capabilities. Each entry includes the startup's domain, a brief description, and specific examples of how they use agentic AI and automation, suitable for inclusion in your book on AI enablement.

1. Moveworks

- Domain: Enterprise Automation, IT, and HR Support
  - Description: Moveworks provides an AI-powered platform that automates enterprise workflows, focusing on IT support, HR, and employee services.
  - How They Use Agentic AI and Automation:

Moveworks' agentic AI integrates autonomous goal-setting, reasoning, and execution to handle complex tasks like resolving IT tickets or answering HR queries. For example, their AI assistant, HelpBot, proactively pulls data from multiple systems to resolve issues such as password resets or software access requests without human intervention.

At Palo Alto Networks, Moveworks' AI agent "Sheldon" supports a hybrid workforce by answering employee queries on benefits and policies conversationally, leveraging Natural Language Understanding (NLU) to provide context-aware responses in seconds.

The platform uses Retrieval-Augmented Generation (RAG) and cross-system integrations to enhance decision-making, automating over 1,000 hours of complex tasks for companies like PowerDesign.

2. Beam AI

- Domain: Business Process Automation

Description: Beam AI offers a platform for Agentic Process Automation, providing AI agents to streamline business processes across industries like insurance and healthcare.

- How They Use Agentic AI and Automation:

Beam AI's AI Agent Hub allows businesses to manage multiple AI agents that automate workflows, such as claims processing or patient data management. For instance, in insurance, their agents autonomously verify claims by pulling data from disparate sources and making decisions based on predefined rules. The platform includes pre-trained templates and customizable integrations, enabling rapid deployment of automation solutions tailored to specific business needs, such as automating customer onboarding in healthcare.

- Recent developments include expanding industry-specific solutions and enhancing enterprise-grade security to ensure compliance and data protection.

3. Hippocratic AI

- Domain: Healthcare
- Description: Hippocratic AI develops AI agents to assist with healthcare tasks, aiming to outperform human nurses in specific functions at a lower cost.
  - How They Use Agentic AI and Automation:

Their AI agents handle tasks like patient communication, appointment scheduling, and triage, costing $9/hour compared to $60.26/hour for a registered nurse in California. For example, an agent can autonomously manage patient inquiries, schedule appointments, and update electronic health records (EHRs).

Partnered with NVIDIA, Hippocratic AI developed super-low-latency "empathy inference" to enable natural, empathetic patient interactions, enhancing patient experience.

They launched a staffing marketplace for hiring AI agents and are in phase three of safety testing with 5,000 nurses and 500 physicians, automating workflows across 40+ provider groups.

4. Aisera

- Domain: Intelligent Service Automation, Customer Service, IT Management
- Description: Aisera provides AI-driven solutions for customer service and IT service desk automation, enhancing enterprise efficiency.
- How They Use Agentic AI and Automation:

Aisera's agentic AI automates IT service management and customer interactions by leveraging continuous learning from user feedback. For example, their AI service desk autonomously resolves routine IT requests, such as software installations, by integrating with enterprise systems.Their customer experience automation tools use real-time analytics to provide insights, enabling proactive support. In retail, Aisera's agents handle customer inquiries across channels, reducing resolution times by autonomously retrieving answers from knowledge bases.The platform supports multi-domain automation, streamlining processes in HR, sales, and customer service with predictive intelligence.

5. Adept AI

- **Domain**: Enterprise Productivity, Workflow Automation
- **Description**: Founded in 2022, Adept AI builds agentic AI that interacts with computer interfaces to automate enterprise workflows, acting as an AI co-worker.
- **How They Use Agentic AI and Automation**: Adept's AI agents respond to natural-language commands to control desktop applications, automating tasks like email processing for recruiters or invoice handling for account managers. For example, an agent can autonomously extract data from invoices, verify it, and update financial systems.Their platform enables businesses to deploy custom agents that integrate with existing software, streamlining workflows in healthcare admin (e.g., patient record management) and finance.Adept Experiments showcases enterprise applications, demonstrating how agents can handle repetitive tasks to boost productivity.

6. Relevance AI

- **Domain**: No-Code AI Development, Business Automation
- **Description**: Relevance AI provides a no-code platform for businesses to build custom AI agents, empowering non-technical users to automate workflows.
- **How They Use Agentic AI and Automation:**

Their platform allows Fortune 500 companies to create AI agents for tasks like healthcare administrative automation (e.g., patient scheduling) in minutes. For instance, a hospital can deploy an agent to manage appointment reminders and follow-ups without coding.Relevance AI uses Retrieval-Augmented Generation (RAG) to ensure data-driven, accurate responses, ideal for processing diverse data types in real time.Recently raised $18 million to expand its platform, enabling businesses to automate complex workflows like document categorization and sentiment analysis.

7. Darktrace

- **Domain**: Cybersecurity
- **Description**: Darktrace leverages agentic AI to provide real-time cybersecurity solutions, protecting enterprises from complex cyber threats.
- **How They Use Agentic AI and Automation:**
- Darktrace's AI agents continuously monitor network traffic 24/7, autonomously detecting suspicious patterns and responding to threats by isolating impacted systems or alerting teams. For example, their algorithms, modeled on the human immune system, identify previously unseen cyberattacks in real time.The platform automates threat mitigation, reducing response times and minimizing potential damage, ensuring long-term security for organizations.Their agentic AI adapts to evolving cyber threats, learning from new patterns to improve detection accuracy.

8. Penciled

- Domain: Healthcare
- **Description**: Penciled, a US-based startup, develops an AI assistant, Nicole, for healthcare administrative tasks, focusing on patient communication.
- **How They Use Agentic AI and Automation**:Nicole automates HIPAA-compliant texts and calls to multiple patients simultaneously, handling tasks like scheduling, updating, or canceling appointments. For example, it can fill last-minute cancellations by autonomously contacting waitlisted patients.The AI integrates with electronic health records (EHRs), streamlining data management and reducing administrative workload, allowing medical staff to focus on patient care.Nicole's human-like voice and multilingual capabilities enhance patient experience and operational efficiency.

9. Brance

- **Domain**: Sales Automation, Hospitality, Automotive
- **Description**: Brance, an Indian startup, develops generative AI agents to accelerate sales conversions in industries like hospitality and automotive.
- **How They Use Agentic AI and Automation:**

In hospitality, Brance's AI agents answer user queries instantly across multiple channels (e.g., social media), increasing bookings by automating responses and suggesting upsell services based on customer interactions.In automotive, their co-pilot analyzes customer calls, qualifies leads, and tailors follow-up communications, enabling sales teams to focus on high-potential leads.The omnichannel platform reduces response times, improving customer experience and OTA reviews.

10. Enhans

- **Domain**: Retail, E-commerce
- **Description**: Enhans, a South Korean startup, offers CommerceOS, a conversational AI platform for retail market automation.
- **How They Use Agentic AI and Automation:**

CommerceOS uses LLMs to model user behavior and automate customer interactions, such as answering product queries or recommending items based on market trends.The platform implements dynamic pricing and promotional activities autonomously, analyzing real-time market data to optimize product exposure and sales.Enhans' agents streamline e-commerce operations, from catalog updates to customer support, reducing manual intervention.

11. Lindy.ai

Domain: Business Automation, Workflow Management

Description: Lindy.ai offers customizable digital agents, "Lindies," to automate tasks across industries, from document discovery to code creation.

How They Use Agentic AI and Automation:

Lindies handle complex workflows, such as automating document discovery for legal firms or generating code for software development teams. For example, a Lindy can autonomously extract relevant clauses from contracts and summarize them.The platform supports collaborative workflows, where multiple agents work together to complete tasks like project management or customer onboarding.Lindy.ai's flexibility allows businesses to tailor agents to specific needs, enhancing productivity in healthcare and finance.

12. AutoGPT

Domain: General Automation, AI Development

Description: AutoGPT is an open-source platform using large language models to execute complex tasks autonomously, evolving toward user-friendly interfaces.

How They Use Agentic AI and Automation:

AutoGPT's agents break down tasks into subtasks, autonomously planning and executing them. For example, a business can use AutoGPT to automate market research by having the agent collect data, analyze trends, and generate reports.The platform is developing a graphical interface to make advanced AI tools accessible to non-technical users, such as healthcare admins automating patient data analysis.Its rapid popularity highlights its potential to drive automation across domains like e-commerce and education.

13. CrewAI

- **Domain**: Multi-Agent Automation, Workflow Optimization
- **Description**: CrewAI provides a platform for building and deploying multi-agent automation workflows using any large language model (LLM).
- **How They Use Agentic AI and Automation:**

CrewAI's platform enables businesses to create multi-agent systems for tasks like supply chain optimization. For example, in logistics, agents can autonomously manage inventory, reconfigure delivery routes, and source alternative suppliers in response to disruptions.The four-step process (Build, Deploy, Track, Iterate) ensures rapid deployment and continuous improvement, with tools for monitoring and refining agent performance.CrewAI integrates with various apps and supports human-in-the-loop feedback, making it ideal for industries like manufacturing and retail.

14. Orby AI

- **Domain**: Enterprise Automation
- **Description**: Orby AI leverages Generative Process Automation (GPA) to enhance enterprise efficiency, focusing on context-aware automation.
- **How They Use Agentic AI and Automation:** Orby AI's platform uses a multimodal Large Action Model (LAM) to understand context and automate complex workflows, such as financial reporting or supply chain

management. For example, an agent can autonomously generate audit-ready financial reports by analyzing data from multiple sources.Their AI agents learn from team interactions, mimicking experienced employees to improve decision-making over time.Orby AI's neuro-symbolic programming ensures high accuracy in tasks like data validation and compliance checks.

15. ScreenMate AI

- **Domain**: Web Automation, E-commerce, Customer Support
- **Description**: ScreenMate AI automates web-based tasks using simple text instructions, transforming them into actionable workflows.
- **How They Use Agentic AI and Automation:**

ScreenMate AI automates e-commerce tasks like keeping catalogs and prices updated by autonomously scraping web data and updating databases. For example, it can adjust product prices based on competitor analysis.In customer support, the platform streamlines onboarding by automating form filling and data collection, reducing response times.It also supports UI testing by simulating user interactions, ensuring seamless web application performance.

These examples explore how emerging startups are revolutionizing industries by leveraging agentic AI—intelligent systems that operate with autonomy, make contextual decisions, and collaborate seamlessly with humans. From cybersecurity to healthcare and retail, these startups are deploying AI agents that go beyond automation to solve complex, real-world problems with precision.

It highlights five core themes:

- Autonomy in Action: Startups are embracing adaptive AI agents that make real-time decisions, moving beyond static rules (e.g., Darktrace, Aisera).
- Domain-Centric Innovation: AI is being tailored to verticals like healthcare (Hippocratic AI), cybersecurity, and retail, solving sector-specific challenges.
- Scalable Integration: Tools like Beam AI and CrewAI enable rapid, enterprise-grade AI deployment, blending with existing workflows.
- Human-AI Synergy: Pioneers like Moveworks and Adept AI are showing how AI can empower—not replace—human teams.
- Cost-Productivity Edge: Startups achieve operational efficiency by dramatically lowering costs and unlocking human capacity for strategic growth.

These insights offer a roadmap for startups aiming to scale smartly and sustainably using cutting-edge, agentic AI.

CHAPTER THREE

Building a Startup with Open Source Everything

Introduction

The biggest myth in the startup world is that building something valuable requires deep pockets. In reality, today's most powerful startups are being built not with millions in venture capital, but with free tools, open ecosystems, and AI superpowers.

The open-source movement has evolved far beyond just software. Today, a startup can be bootstrapped entirely on the back of free, open, and community-driven tools — from infrastructure to branding.

Let's break down how you can build an entire company without spending a fortune — and sometimes without spending anything at all.

This chapter shows you how to replace costly software subscriptions and proprietary tech with powerful, collaborative alternatives.

3.1 Why Open Source Is a Startup Superpower

- Cost savings: Free or low-cost licenses
- Customizability: You control the code and roadmap
- Community Support: Fast problem solving, innovation at scale
- Transparency: Know exactly what your tools do
- Security: Constantly audited by a global developer base

3.2 Core Open Source Stack for Every Startup

Here's a powerful list of free and open-source tools across various business functions that can help startups do more with less — including a few surprising and underused gems:

1. Marketing & Customer Engagement

Mautic: Open-source marketing automation (email campaigns, drip campaigns, lead scoring).

Chatwoot: Customer support chat platform with multi-channel support (website, WhatsApp, etc.).

PostHog: Product analytics alternative to Mixpanel, supports user behavior tracking and heatmaps.

Listmonk: High-performance email newsletter and campaign tool, self-hosted.

2. Research & Analytics

Metabase: Business intelligence and data visualization for teams (SQL & non-SQL users).

Jupyter Notebooks: Ideal for data science, analytics, and documentation with code.

Scrapy: Python framework for building powerful web scrapers for competitive research.

3. Website, Sales & Support

EspoCRM: Lightweight CRM to manage sales pipelines, customers, and workflows.

Zammad: A powerful helpdesk/support ticketing system with email and chat integration.

Grav: A fast, flexible flat-file CMS for building websites without databases.

4. Recruitment & HR

OrangeHRM: A full-featured open-source Human Resource Management system.

Odoo (Community Edition): Includes apps for HR, recruitment, payroll, CRM, invoicing, and more.

5. Office & Remote Work

Jitsi Meet: Secure, open-source video conferencing (alternative to Zoom/Google Meet).

OnlyOffice / LibreOffice: Microsoft Office alternatives with collaboration features.

Mattermost / Rocket.Chat: Self-hosted Slack alternatives with team messaging and bot support.

6. Project & Task Management

Taiga: Scrum/Kanban-based project management tool with beautiful UI.

OpenProject: Comprehensive tool for project planning, scheduling, task tracking.

Wekan: Simple Kanban board similar to Trello, good for lightweight task tracking.

7. Programming & Development

VS Code (open-source fork: VSCodium): Lightweight, extensible code editor.

GitLab CE: Full DevOps lifecycle management including Git repo, CI/CD, and issue tracking.

Gitea: Lightweight Git hosting solution, ideal for small teams.

8. Presentations & Visuals

Reveal.js: HTML presentation framework for creating sleek, interactive slides.

Excalidraw: Open-source hand-drawn-style diagram tool, great for ideation.

Penpot: Design and prototyping tool (open-source Figma alternative).

9. AI & Automation Tools

Haystack: Open-source framework for building NLP-powered search, QA systems.

Rasa: Build your own AI chatbots and virtual assistants with custom NLP models.

Auto-GPT / AgentGPT: Early open-source attempts at autonomous GPT-powered task agents.

10. Surprising & Super Useful

Obsidian (with open plugins): Powerful markdown knowledge base for notes, ideas, and strategy.

TimeShift: Time-tracking and productivity analysis for individuals or teams.

Draw.io / diagrams.net: Great for flowcharts, org charts, architecture diagrams.

The following table gives the summary of various open source tools available along with corresponding use cases across different functional areas of the startups.

Function	Open Source Tool	Use Case
Operating System	Ubuntu / Fedora	Secure, reliable base
Development Platform	GitLab / Gitea	Code repo + CI/CD
Website Builder	Hugo / Astro / WordPress	Build and host site
Frontend Builder	Appsmith / Budibase	Drag-and-drop UI builder
Backend API	Supabase / PocketBase / Hasura	Scalable DB + Auth
Design & Prototyping	Penpot	Open-source Figma
CRM	EspoCRM / Yetiforce	Manage customers
Project Mgmt	Taiga / Plane / OpenProject	Agile workflows
Marketing Automation	Mautic	Email, landing pages
Customer Support	Chatwoot / Papercups	Live chat, ticketing
Analytics	Plausible / Matomo	Website traffic insights
Internal Docs	Outline / Logseq	Internal wiki
Video Conferencing	Jitsi Meet	Zoom alternative

Core Opensource Stack for every enterprise

Open-source doesn't mean "limited" — it means "unlocked."

With these tools, you can build scalable, secure, and robust systems without paying enterprise-level fees.

3.3 Leveraging GitHub and Open Ecosystems

- Use GitHub Topics to find "awesome lists" for any function
- Join open-source communities: Discord, Reddit, IndieHackers

- Contribute back: PRs, bug fixes, documentation — build visibility
- Fork and customize code to suit your product

3.4 Cloud Credits and Startup Programs

Cloud computing has leveled the playing field. You no longer need to own servers or manage complex infrastructure.

Cloud giants are offering generous credits and resources to startups:

AWS Activate: Up to $100,000 in credits for eligible startups.

Google Cloud for Startups: $2,000 to $200,000 in credits.

Microsoft for Startups Founders Hub: Free access to Azure, GitHub Copilot, OpenAI APIs, and mentorship.

Replit's Bounties & Startup Hub: Code in the cloud and even earn while building.

These programs don't just give you access to cloud infrastructure — they offer free tools, AI APIs, mentorship, legal support, and go-to-market resources.

If you're smart about signing up and using these credits wisely, your first 12–18 months of infrastructure could cost ₹0.

3.5 Success Stories Built on Open Source

- Ghost: Publishing platform, now doing millions in revenue
- PostHog: Open-source product analytics

- Mattermost: Slack alternative used by enterprises
- Redash: Acquired by Databricks — data dashboarding
- Each started lean, iterated fast, and scaled through the strength of community and open access.

3.6 Framework: OS-LAUNCH

- OS-LAUNCH is a model to build your startup stack in 7 steps:
- Operating system — Ubuntu for DevOps, Windows Subsystem for Linux
- Software stack — Select based on your product (SaaS, marketplace, etc.)
- Low-code tools — Appsmith, Budibase for speed
- Analytics — Set up early using Plausible or Matomo
- User workflows — Automate CRM/email with Mautic
- Navigation — Plan & manage using Taiga or Plane
- Chat, help, and docs — Chatwoot + Outline

3.7 Free LLMs and AI Frameworks

A few years ago, advanced AI models like GPT-3 or BERT were locked behind paywalls or restricted access. Today, we live in an open AI revolution:

- Mistral, LLaMA 3, Gemma, and Claude offer high-performance large language models for free or open licensing.
- Frameworks like LangChain, LlamaIndex, and Haystack help you build production-ready AI apps — from

chatbots to custom agents — with minimal code.

- You can build, fine-tune, and deploy your own LLMs locally or in the cloud using open-source alternatives to proprietary APIs.
- Voice AI, image generation, translation, summarization, sentiment analysis — all can be done using freely available models and frameworks.
- You no longer need to buy intelligence — you can borrow it, fine-tune it, or create it with open tools.

3.8 Tips for Success

- Start simple: Use minimum tools and scale as needed
- Stay updated: Follow GitHub stars, changelogs, Reddit
- Backup and monitor: Use open-source backup & alert tools like BorgBackup or Uptime Kuma
- Train team/agents: Use AI to generate SOPs and training from open-source tool docs

Takeaway

Open source is no longer just an alternative — it's often the better choice. From dev to deployment, every part of your startup can be run on battle-tested tools built by thousands around the world, at zero cost to you.

As we've seen, today's startups face enormous challenges—tight resources, high competition, and rising operational costs. Yet, they also possess something incredibly powerful: access to groundbreaking technologies that were once the domain of tech giants and research labs.

Agentic AI, open-source large language models (LLMs), and immersive Metaverse tools have leveled the playing field for early-stage founders with a bold vision.

Agentic AI is redefining what it means to automate. No longer confined to scripted rules, these systems think, adapt, and act in real time—empowering startups to function with the agility of a large enterprise. Whether it's deploying autonomous cybersecurity agents like Darktrace or enabling 24/7 intelligent customer support with Aisera, AI is becoming the co-founder every startup needs.

Moreover, these innovations are not generic. Startups are using domain-specific models and frameworks—like Hippocratic AI in healthcare or Enhans in retail—to solve unique problems with uncanny precision. The flexibility and scalability of platforms like Beam AI and CrewAI allow seamless integration with existing systems, ensuring that even small teams can rapidly deploy world-class solutions.

Crucially, these technologies foster a hybrid operating model—where AI does the heavy lifting, and human insight guides critical decisions. This synergy doesn't just improve efficiency—it unlocks new realms of productivity, enabling startup founders to focus on creativity, strategy, and impact.

And perhaps most importantly for cash-strapped entrepreneurs, agentic AI and open-source LLMs offer tremendous cost efficiency. AI agents can now perform tasks at a fraction of the traditional cost (as little as $9/hour in healthcare versus $60/hour for human alternatives), while still allowing human experts to step in when necessary.

What's Next

In the chapters that follow, we'll dive into the specific technologies and open-source tools that are fueling this revolution. You'll discover powerful Free LLMs that rival commercial giants, open-source AI agent frameworks that can transform workflows, and Metaverse platforms that offer new ways to engage customers and build digital-first businesses.

This is your roadmap to turning bold startup dreams into scalable, sustainable, and smart ventures—without burning a hole in your wallet.

Let's explore the future, one open-source tool at a time.

CHAPTER FOUR

Training Your AI Army — Agents That Work for You

Introduction

What if you could build a team of digital employees — researchers, analysts, content writers, marketers, coders, and even project managers — all powered by AI, all working 24/7, and all free or low-cost? That's the promise of AI agents.

This chapter explores how startup founders can deploy and orchestrate AI agents using open-source frameworks, freeing themselves from operational grind and unlocking hyper-efficiency.

AI Agents – Your First Virtual Team

Imagine this: It's 2 a.m. You're exhausted. Your to-do list is untouched. You need to do customer support, research competitors, prepare a product brief, and send a proposal to a client in another timezone. Now imagine all of that gets done — not by a team of five — but by an autonomous AI agent you trained in a weekend.

Welcome to the world of **agentic AI.**

Agentic AI is a class of artificial intelligence that focuses on autonomous systems that can make decisions and perform tasks without human intervention. The independent systems automatically respond to conditions, to produce process results.

4.1 What Are AI Agents?

AI Agents are autonomous software programs powered by large language models (LLMs) and tools that can reason, plan, execute tasks, and collaborate with other agents or humans.

An AI agent is not just a chatbot. It's a piece of software that can reason, plan, and act on your behalf. Powered by large language models like LLaMA 3 or Mistral, and frameworks like LangChain, CrewAI, and AutoGen, these agents can:

- Search the internet for specific information
- Fill out forms and respond to emails
- Generate documents and marketing content
- Book meetings and follow up with leads
- Write code, debug, and explain concepts
- Even monitor and train other agents

4.1.1: Types of AI Agents:

AI agents are transforming how startups and enterprises operate, acting as tireless digital co-workers that think, decide, and act with context and intelligence. Let's explore how agentic AI is shaping the next wave of innovation across industries:

i) Voice Agents – Conversational Intelligence

Voice-driven AI agents, powered by platforms like ElevenLabs and Vapi, are revolutionizing customer engagement. These systems understand spoken language, interpret intent, and deliver human-like responses. Whether it's handling support calls, onboarding customers, or managing bookings, voice agents deliver faster, more empathetic, and scalable interactions.

ii) Computer Use Agents – Your AI Desktop Colleague

Agents powered by models like Claude and ChatGPT can now operate your desktop for you—navigating browsers, editing documents, switching apps, and even remembering past tasks. These AI copilots act as true digital workers, freeing users from repetitive tasks and enabling focus on strategic decision-making.

iii) Coding Agents – Engineering at Light Speed

Specialized agents such as CURSOR and Roo Code are redefining software development. These intelligent assistants not only write and debug code but also understand business logic, helping developers move from concept to deployment exponentially faster. They're the new productivity superpower for modern dev teams.

iv) Agentic RAG – Knowledge on Demand

Combining the power of Retrieval-Augmented Generation, tools like Perplexity and Glean deliver precise, real-time answers from vast data repositories. These agents don't guess—they know, because they retrieve and generate contextually rich, source-backed insights critical for decision-making.

v) Workflow Automation Agents – Business Without Friction

Platforms like n8n and Tines enable AI agents to orchestrate complex business workflows. These agents integrate APIs, respond to triggers, and automate multi-step processes across departments—reducing errors, saving time, and boosting operational efficiency.

vi) Tool-Specific Agents – Purpose-Built Precision

Focused agents such as Breez, Clay, or Kogi are engineered for specific applications—like search, CRM, or email. These agents provide laser-focused automation and intelligence tailored to high-ROI tasks, offering deep value with minimal setup.

4.1.2 Categories of AI Agents with examples

<u>Enterprise AI Agent Categories</u>

- Business Intelligence AI Agents – These agents help companies analyze vast data sets to generate actionable insights, detect trends, and improve decision-making.
- Operations AI Agents – Focused on streamlining workflows, optimizing resources, and predicting maintenance needs to boost operational efficiency.
- Cybersecurity AI Agents – Designed to detect threats, monitor for anomalies, and automate responses to enhance security across enterprise systems.
- HR & Talent AI Agents – These agents assist in hiring, employee performance analysis, retention strategies, and internal mobility management.
- IT Operations (AIOps) Agents – Help detect incidents, automate resolutions, and manage complex infrastructure across cloud and on-premise environments.
- Finance AI Agents – Provide support in fraud detection, risk analysis, financial forecasting, and invoice/expense management.
- Compliance AI Agents – Automate audit processes, track policy adherence, and monitor regulatory compliance.

- Legal AI Agents – Assist in document review, contract analysis, legal research, and due diligence.

B2B AI Agent Categories

- Sales Intelligence Agents – Used by B2B companies to identify leads, score them, segment customers, and forecast sales performance.
- Customer Support AI Agents – AI-driven chatbots and assistants that offer multilingual support, FAQs, and self-service to enterprise clients.
- Procurement AI Agents – Streamline vendor selection, negotiate contracts, and optimize procurement spend using historical data.
- Partner Management Agents – Aid in onboarding new partners, tracking their performance, and facilitating co-marketing activities.
- Marketing Automation Agents – Optimize ad campaigns, automate email follow-ups, and analyze engagement across channels.
- Supply Chain & Logistics Agents – Enhance inventory forecasting, delivery tracking, and route optimization.

B2C AI Agent Categories

- Virtual Shopping Assistants – Help consumers find the right products, compare prices, and offer personalized recommendations.
- B2C Customer Support Agents – Provide 24/7 customer assistance, handle returns, complaints, and service queries in real-time.
- Healthcare AI Agents – Offer services like symptom checking, telehealth scheduling, medication reminders,

and health tracking.

- Finance & Budgeting Agents – Help users manage personal finance by tracking spending, suggesting savings, and financial planning.
- Education & Learning Agents – Provide personalized tutoring, learning paths, and preparation assistance for exams and certifications.
- Entertainment Recommendation Agents – Recommend movies, music, podcasts, and games based on user preferences and history.
- Fitness & Wellness Agents – Create tailored workout plans, track diet and health metrics, and monitor mental well-being.
- Travel & Booking Agents – Help users plan trips, book flights/hotels, provide price alerts, and manage travel itineraries.

4.2 Why Startups Should Use AI Agents

- Replace repetitive roles: Research, reporting, scheduling, drafting
- Save hiring cost: No salaries, insurance, or onboarding
- 24/7 operations: No downtime, timezone-proof teams
- Scale fast: Clone agents instead of hiring
- Specialized expertise: Train domain-specific agents (e.g., legal, sales, tech)

What You Need to Build One

You don't need a data center or a PhD. Here's a starter stack to deploy your own AI agent:

- LLM (Large Language Model): Ollama lets you run LLaMA 3 locally for free

- Framework: LangChain or CrewAI
- Interface: A simple Streamlit or Telegram bot
- Agent Tools: File access, browser, calculator, custom APIs

Example: Your AI Researcher Agent

Python Program to Research Competitors using an AI Agent

```
from langchain.agents import initialize_agent, Tool
from langchain.llms import Ollama
llm = Ollama(model="llama3")
tools = [Tool(name="Search", func=web_search_function)]
agent = initialize_agent(tools, llm, agent="zero-shot-react-description")
response = agent.run("Summarize the top 5 competitors of my product.")
print(response)
```

Use Cases in Real Startups

- A legal-tech startup built an agent to summarize court judgments
- A SaaS company uses an agent to generate code documentation
- A fashion brand automates influencer outreach through agents

4.3 The Open Source Agent Stack

The following table presents a comparative overview of leading open-source frameworks that enable startups and developers to build AI agents capable of autonomous reasoning, task execution, and real-time decision-making. Whether you're developing a smart customer support bot, a workflow automation agent, or a personal productivity assistant, these frameworks—such as LangChain, CrewAI, AutoGen, and MetaGPT—offer customizable and modular options to design multi-agent systems tailored to specific startup needs.

Each framework is assessed across key dimensions:

- Ease of Use: Developer-friendly APIs and documentation.
- Extensibility: Ability to integrate tools, plugins, or new LLMs.
- Multi-Agent Coordination: Support for task delegation and collaboration between agents.
- Integration Flexibility: Compatibility with third-party APIs, tools, and enterprise systems.
- Use Cases: Suggested applications from customer support to complex RAG (Retrieval Augmented Generation) pipelines.

These platforms democratize the power of agentic AI, allowing even small teams to build highly intelligent systems without starting from scratch or paying for expensive proprietary platforms.

Framework	Description	Best For
LangChain	Framework for building LLM-based apps	Orchestration, tool use
CrewAI	Multi-agent collaboration	Task planning, teamwork
AutoGen (Microsoft)	Agent-to-agent conversation framework	Complex coordination
SuperAgent	Task automation pipelines	E2E automation
Flowise	Visual drag-and-drop LLM apps	No-code agent building
OpenAgents	Browser-based, tool-using agents	Web tasks, API work

You can use **Ollama + Mistral** locally to power these agents *offline* if needed.

The Opensource AI Agent stack

4.4 Agent Roles for a Startup

As startups juggle limited resources and tight deadlines, AI agents can serve as digital team members—automating repetitive tasks, accelerating decision-making, and freeing up founders to focus on strategy and innovation. Below is a breakdown of key startup functions that can be represented and enhanced by autonomous AI agents:

1. Marketing Agent

- Role: Plans and executes marketing campaigns, schedules social media posts, analyzes performance metrics.
- AI Use: Auto-generates content (e.g., blog posts, LinkedIn updates), A/B testing ideas, SEO recommendations.
- Tools: LangChain + OpenAI/Mistral, integrated with Zapier/HubSpot.

2. Research Agent

- Role: Continuously scans the internet for competitive intel, market trends, regulatory changes, and new technologies.
- AI Use: Performs real-time web search, summarizes PDFs or reports, recommends strategies.
- Tools: AutoGen or CrewAI + Browsing plugins (like Tavily, Serper).

3. Customer Service Agent

- Role: Handles customer queries, support tickets, onboarding, and feedback collection.
- AI Use: Trained on startup FAQs or manuals to provide 24/7 contextual support.
- Tools: LangChain + VectorDB (e.g., Chroma/Weaviate), integrated with platforms like WhatsApp, Telegram, or web chat.

4. Product Manager Agent

- Role: Helps prioritize product features, analyze customer pain points, and simulate user stories.
- AI Use: Connects feedback to product roadmap, drafts PRDs (Product Requirement Documents), compares competitors.
- Tools: CrewAI for task delegation, integrated with Notion, Jira, or Trello.

5. Finance & Admin Agent

- Role: Tracks expenses, forecasts cash flow, helps with compliance documentation, and even manages investor reports.
- AI Use: Scans receipts, automates reporting, manages reminders for legal/tax filings.
- Tools: LangChain + Google Sheets plugin + document parsers like Unstructured.io.

6. Developer Agent

- Role: Assists with coding tasks, suggests code snippets, debugs errors, and documents APIs.

- AI Use: Co-programming with tools like Code Interpreter, GitHub Copilot, or a local Mistral-powered coder agent.
- Tools: OpenDevin, MetaGPT, or a fine-tuned agent via Ollama.

7. Hiring & HR Agent

- Role: Screens resumes, schedules interviews, and manages onboarding.
- AI Use: Filters candidate profiles, summarizes CVs, and automates follow-ups.
- Tools: LangChain + ResumeParser + email integrations.

The following table summarises the important agents and their roles.

Role	Description	Tools
Research Agent	Finds trends, summaries, competitors	CrewAI + Web search tools
Content Agent	Writes blog posts, newsletters, ads	LangChain + GPT-J or Mistral
Sales Agent	Crafts cold emails, follow-ups, lead scoring	Flowise + CRM
Marketing Agent	Suggests SEO, ad copy, social posts	SuperAgent + OpenAPI
Tech Agent	Writes code, unit tests, bug detection	Codeium + AutoGen
PM Agent	Updates tasks, reminds you, sets timelines	CrewAI + Notion API
HR Agent	Pre-screens resumes, drafts JD	LangChain + ATS
Customer Agent	Handles queries, FAQs, escalations	Chatwoot + LLM backend

Your Digital Co-Founders

Bottom Line

Each of these agents acts as a digital co-founder or virtual team member, providing specialized support in areas that typically drain time and budget. By deploying such agents early on, startups can drastically improve their operational efficiency, maintain lean teams, and still scale faster with precision.

4.5 Building Your First Agent

Let's say you want a Content Writing Agent:

Use LangChain with a Mistral model via Ollama

Give it a goal: "Create 3 SEO-friendly blog posts per week"

Add tools: serpapi for Google search, openai for generation

Add memory to track past topics

Test it with prompts: "Write a 500-word article on AI in agriculture"

Boom — your first employee.

Once you've deployed one agent, you can start orchestrating multiple agents into a team. Imagine:

- One agent researching your market
- Another writing cold emails
- A third analyzing feedback
- And a fourth summarizing team meetings

Together, they become your first virtual team — always-on, cost-free, and infinitely scalable.

4.6 Orchestrating a Team of Agents

With Crew AI, you can:

- Assign roles and personalities
- Set task sequences (planner → researcher → writer → reviewer)
- Create workflows like a real startup team

- Use tools and memory for continuity

Goal: Launch a product landing page

- Agent 1: Market research
- Agent 2: Copywriting
- Agent 3: UI Design suggestions
- Agent 4: SEO check
- Agent 5: Publish via Framer API

4.7 AI Agent Deployment Tips

- Keep them focused: Single-domain agents work better
- Monitor output: Humans should still review critical work
- Use secure environments: Especially for agents with access to APIs or databases
- Continual learning: Feed your agents documentation, SOPs, or feedback
- Link to your CRM/project tools: Use Zapier or custom APIs

4.8 Pitfalls to Avoid

- Over-automation: Some things still need human empathy
- No supervision: Always have a review loop
- Bad prompt design: Garbage in, garbage out
- Data privacy: Ensure sensitive info isn't exposed

Takeaway

AI agents are your leanest team members — fast, tireless, and scalable. By building a smart AI army, you give your startup unfair leverage without increasing your burn rate. The future isn't hiring more — it's orchestrating better.

CHAPTER FIVE

ENTER THE METAVERSE — WORK, MEET, AND SELL IN 3D

Introduction

The Metaverse is no longer just a buzzword. It's evolving into a platform that can help startups build immersive brand experiences, redefine remote work, and even sell directly to customers in innovative ways. This chapter explains how startups can harness the power of the Metaverse to gain a competitive edge, engage with customers, and collaborate efficiently.

5.1 What Is the Metaverse and Why Does It Matter to Startups?

The Metaverse is a shared virtual space, created by the convergence of virtually enhanced physical reality and persistent digital worlds. It combines augmented reality

(AR), virtual reality (VR), 3D environments, and blockchain to create an immersive experience.

.? Virtual Offices, Expos, and Demos

In the new digital era, your "office" no longer needs a zip code. Platforms like Gather, Spatial, Virbela, and Mozilla Hubs let you create 3D virtual offices that simulate real-world collaboration — complete with meeting rooms, whiteboards, and watercooler chats. You can walk through an office, attend a virtual trade expo, or deliver product demos to clients in immersive 3D environments — all from your laptop.

?? How to Create Your First Room

Creating your first virtual space is easy. Platforms like Gather or Spatial offer templates for offices, booths, or auditoriums. You start by selecting a layout, customizing your avatar, and embedding interactive elements like screen-sharing zones, slides, or video feeds. No coding needed — it's drag-and-drop.

? Integrating Bots and Immersive Experiences

Bring your space to life with AI bots and interactive layers. Integrate virtual assistants using ChatGPT or CrewAI to greet visitors, answer questions, or conduct onboarding tours. Use immersive tools like 3D product showcases, AR filters, or gamified experiences to increase engagement. You can even plug in CRM systems or collect lead data directly inside the virtual room.

This isn't the metaverse of tomorrow — it's your startup showroom today.

For startups, the Metaverse can offer:

- Brand Immersion: A new way to engage customers, offering interactive 3D spaces.
- Remote Collaboration: Virtual offices and workspaces that feel more engaging than video calls.
- New Sales Channels: Selling virtual goods or offering services in 3D environments.
- Global Reach: You can host events and sell products to a worldwide audience without geographical constraints.

5.2 The Different Facets of the Metaverse for Startups

The Metaverse is not just a futuristic playground—it is fast becoming a practical innovation arena where startups can build immersive experiences, create new digital economies, and enhance real-world engagement through virtual layers.

The Metaverse is emerging as a critical enabler for immersive digital innovation. For startups, it offers a multidimensional canvas to rethink how people work, learn, socialize, and shop. Each "facet" of the Metaverse opens a specific strategic frontier, combining AI, blockchain, spatial computing, and real-time engagement.

Below is a a list of real use cases, examples, and tools startups can immediately begin using.

Use Case	Example	Tools & Platforms
Virtual Offices	Work from anywhere in a 3D collaborative space	Spatial, Horizon Workrooms, FrameVR
Customer Engagement	Product demos, brand experiences, virtual stores	Decentraland, Somnium Space, Roblox
Events & Conferences	Host immersive product launches, webinars, or expos	AltspaceVR, Gather, Hopin
Product Development	Visualize products in 3D, offer user-generated designs	Blender, Tinkercad, Unity
E-commerce	Virtual showrooms, virtual goods, and NFT marketplaces	OpenSea, Decentraland Marketplace

Key use cases of Metaverse for Startups

For startups, understanding and leveraging different facets of the Metaverse can unlock unprecedented opportunities for innovation, monetization, and user engagement. These facets represent the building blocks of a parallel digital world that intersects with our physical and virtual realities.

Startups don't need massive budgets to enter the Metaverse—thanks to open-source tools, no-code platforms, and cloud-based rendering engines, they can experiment, prototype, and scale their offerings affordably.

The metaverse is best understood as a stack of complementary facets—each one a technical building block that unlocks a different business opportunity. Start-ups do not have to master everything at once; they can select the facet that solves an immediate pain-point and layer others in later.

Below is a narrative tour through those facets, illustrated with real use cases, early-stage examples, and the mostly free tools you can try today.

1. Immersive visualisation (VR).

This is the head-mounted, fully 3-D side of the metaverse. Brands already create virtual showrooms, universities run digital campuses, and therapists deliver exposure therapy here. Two-person studio Spatial hosts NFT galleries, while Labster sells virtual science labs to schools. You can prototype similar spaces with free tiers of Unity, Unreal Engine, browser-based Mozilla Hubs or FrameVR, and open-source Godot; a single Meta Quest headset often covers the hardware need.

2. Augmented reality (AR).

AR overlays digital objects on the physical world via phones or smart glasses. Start-ups use it for "try-before-you-buy" furniture, field-service instructions that float over machinery, or gamified city-wide treasure hunts. IKEA Place began with Apple's free ARKit, while plant-care app PlantIn diagnoses leaf disease with ARCore. Launch quickly with ARCore/ARKit, 8th Wall, Niantic Lightship, or no-code ZapWorks.

3. Persistent shared worlds.

Always-on browser worlds such as Gather or Topia continue evolving after you log off, giving small teams a virtual HQ, musicians a festival site, or founders a 24/7 hackathon venue. Because they run in WebGL, guests enter with a single link—no headset required.

4. Digital twins.

A digital twin is a live, data-linked replica of a machine, building, patient, or process. Micro-factories use twins for predictive maintenance, hospitals simulate treatment responses, and cities optimise traffic in real time. Open-source FIWARE, Microsoft's free-tier Azure Digital Twins, or Blender + CesiumJS let you build one without licence fees.

5. Avatars and presence.

Visual or voice avatars make remote interaction feel human. Start-ups deploy virtual sales reps or influencer personas. AI-driven Soul Machines builds smiling spokes-avatars for banks; anyone can generate cross-app avatars with Ready Player Me and lifelike voices with ElevenLabs or talking-head video from D-ID.

6. Spatial commerce and tokenised economies.

Monetisation in the metaverse centres on paid virtual goods, NFT wearables, leased event space, or subscription-only VR classrooms. Fashion start-up DressX sells AR outfits, while Somnium Space rents virtual land. You can integrate payments with Thirdweb, Polygon, Stripe for WebXR, or the open-source Metaplex stack.

7. Interaction middleware.

Standards such as OpenXR, WebXR, and OpenUSD act as the glue connecting headsets, wallets, and back-end data. Using them, a start-up can let a customer move the same avatar from Zoom into a VR showroom or pull live CRM data into an in-world NPC. NVIDIA's free Omniverse sandbox and HyperCube (which layers MCP-style agent calls onto WebXR) accelerate such integrations.

8. Agentic AI in 3-D.

LLM-powered "non-player characters" make virtual spaces useful, not just pretty. Imagine an in-world tutor that adapts to each learner or a shopping stylist who understands your purchase history. Platforms like Convai, CrewAI, Unity Sentis, or a local Mistral 7B model let a two-person team embed intelligent agents inside VR or browser scenes in days.

<u>How a lean start-up might begin</u>

- Isolate one pain-point. Maybe remote onboarding feels flat.
- Pick the lightest facet. A browser HQ in Gather with Ready Player Me avatars.
- Add AI utility. Drop in a GPT-powered HR bot via Convai.
- Validate ROI. Measure shorter ramp-up times; rent the template to other teams.
- Layer up. Later, integrate digital-twin analytics or AR field manuals.

Founder take-aways

- Start browser-first: most users enter via a link, not a headset.
- Leverage open assets: libraries like Sketchfab slash 3-D costs.
- Design ROI from day one: tie each immersive feature to conversion, retention, or speed-to-competence.
- Embed AI early: agentic NPCs provide immediate, measurable value.

Creating original 3-D models is expensive—professional artists charge hundreds of dollars per asset and weeks of work. Online libraries such as Sketchfab, Poly Haven, CGTrader, and BlenderKit host tens of thousands of ready-made meshes, textures, and animations that creators upload under free-to-use or low-cost licences (CC-0, CC-BY, or a few dollars per download). Instead of paying for custom modelling, a start-up can:

- Search for a needed object—say, an MRI scanner, sneaker, or office chair.
- Download it instantly in standard formats (GLB, FBX, OBJ).
- Import into Unity, Unreal, WebGL, or A-Frame, then re-texture or resize as required.

Result: hours instead of weeks, and often zero cash outlay. By mixing open-library assets with a handful of bespoke hero models, founders can prototype virtual showrooms, training scenes, or product demos at a fraction of traditional 3-D production cost—shifting budget from asset creation to user experience and marketing.

With this facet-by-facet approach, even a two-founder start-up can launch revenue-generating immersive experiences—without giant budgets or AAA game studios.

Deep Dive into Selected Use Cases

1. Virtual Onboarding in Virtual Worlds

A startup can design an onboarding experience in a Mozilla Hubs room where new hires are guided by an AI-powered avatar through company culture, tasks, and tools—reducing time-to-productivity.

2. Retail AR Try-On

A fashion startup can let users virtually try on clothes using 8thWall + Snap Camera, boosting conversion rates and reducing product returns.

3. AI Avatars as Sales Reps

Imagine a digital twin of a luxury car showroom where each customer is greeted by an AI avatar (built on Inworld AI) that explains features, prices, and responds to questions.

4. Metaverse Clinics

Healthtech startups can simulate mental health clinics or therapy environments in VR, using platforms like EngageVR with embedded AI therapists built using GPT + avatar SDKs.

For startups, the Metaverse isn't a luxury—it's a strategic opportunity to differentiate through immersive, intelligent, and decentralized experiences. With open-source and low-code tools, building and scaling such experiences has never been easier.

? Pro Tip: Pair Ollama + Mistral (for offline local LLMs) with lightweight 3D environments like Mozilla Hubs or Unity WebGL exports to build private, secure metaverse applications without depending on cloud APIs.

5.3 How Startups Can Use the Metaverse for Collaboration and Operations

Remote work is changing, and the Metaverse offers new opportunities for startups to make it more engaging and productive.

- **Virtual Workspaces:** Tools like Spatial or Horizon Workrooms offer virtual offices where teams can interact as avatars in a 3D environment, mimicking the feeling of a real office without the geographical constraints.
- **Immersive Collaboration:** Use virtual whiteboards, co-edit documents, and brainstorm as if you were in the same room, with VR tools like Rumii and FrameVR that facilitate a seamless virtual workspace.
- **Team Building:** Organize team-building activities in the Metaverse using VR platforms like AltspaceVR for virtual happy hours or social hangouts, fostering

engagement in ways video calls can't.

5.4 Creating Virtual Customer Experiences

Brands can use the Metaverse to offer new and interactive experiences to customers, including:

- 3D Product Demos: Let customers explore your products in a fully interactive 3D environment, where they can touch, rotate, and even "try on" products virtually (like fashion or home decor).
- Virtual Stores: Brands like Nike and Gucci have set up virtual stores in platforms like Decentraland and Roblox, where users can browse products, interact with displays, and even make purchases in a fully immersive environment.
- Social Shopping: Combine the virtual store with social interaction. Platforms like Somnium Space allow users to interact with friends, attend live events, and shop together, creating a new, fun, and social shopping experience.

5.5 Using the Metaverse for Virtual Events and Networking

- Product Launches & Demos: Imagine hosting a product launch where attendees can walk through a digital showroom, interact with products in real-time, and even chat with product experts, all while using avatars. Platforms like AltspaceVR and Hopin make this possible.

- Networking Events: Traditional conferences and expos are now being replaced by virtual and hybrid experiences. Virtual expos allow visitors to explore booths, interact with hosts, and attend breakout sessions — all from the comfort of their homes.
- Training & Webinars: Offer product training, demos, and webinars in VR, allowing attendees to learn interactively and engage with products. Gather and Virbela are popular platforms for holding virtual training sessions and workshops.

5.6 E-commerce in the Metaverse

Selling in the Metaverse doesn't just mean offering virtual goods. You can:

- Sell real products with immersive experiences: Brands can set up virtual showrooms where customers can walk through an interactive environment, view products, and buy directly.
- NFTs: Non-fungible tokens (NFTs) allow businesses to sell unique digital products (art, music, collectibles, etc.) in the Metaverse. For instance, OpenSea and Rarible are NFT marketplaces that can be integrated into virtual worlds to allow for easy buying and selling.
- Virtual Real Estate: Buy, sell, or rent virtual land within virtual worlds like Decentraland or The Sandbox to showcase your startup or create digital assets that users can purchase.

5.7 Tools and Platforms for Metaverse Creation

To create a Metaverse experience, startups will need access to various tools:

3D Creation & Design Tools:

- Blender: Open-source 3D modeling software for building models and environments.
- Unity: A widely used game engine for creating interactive 3D experiences.
- Tinkercad: Great for beginner 3D design, especially in product prototyping.
- VR Platforms & Social Spaces:
- AltspaceVR: A social VR platform for events, networking, and collaboration.
- Spatial: For creating virtual meeting rooms and immersive collaborative environments.
- Horizon Worlds: Facebook's VR space, which is designed for building communities and businesses.

Metaverse Platforms for Building:

- Decentraland: A decentralized virtual world where users can buy land, build, and create immersive experiences.
- Roblox: A gaming platform that also acts as a Metaverse, with interactive user-generated worlds.
- Somnium Space: A VR world with real estate, social spaces, and content creation capabilities.

5.8 Challenges and Considerations for Startups

While the Metaverse presents exciting opportunities, there are a few challenges startups must consider:

- Tech Requirements: VR headsets and high-speed internet are required to access immersive experiences. This could limit your audience.
- User Adoption: While growing rapidly, the Metaverse is still niche. Your target market may not be fully ready for virtual experiences.
- Development Costs: Creating immersive environments and experiences can be expensive. Startups need to plan for scalability and budget for both short-term and long-term investments.

Takeaway

The Metaverse is the next frontier for startups, offering innovative ways to collaborate, engage customers, and even sell. By integrating immersive virtual environments into your startup's strategy, you can enhance brand presence, foster customer loyalty, and create unique experiences that traditional marketing simply can't offer.

Free Open source LLMs and Metaverse Tools

Here's a curated list of Free & Open-Source tools across:

- LLMs (Large Language Models)
- Agentic AI Frameworks
- Metaverse Platforms

That startups can leverage to build powerful solutions while staying lean:

1. Free & Open-Source LLMs

These can be self-hosted or used via open APIs for NLP, chatbot, or summarization use cases:

- Mistral 7B / Mixtral 8x7B – Powerful open-weight models, great for coding, summarizing, and reasoning tasks.
- LLaMA 2 / LLaMA 3 (Meta) – Available for commercial use (with some conditions); supports chat, reasoning, and Q&A.
- Phi-2 (Microsoft) – Lightweight, great for inference on smaller devices.
- Gemma (Google) – Open weights and efficient; good for chatbot integration.
- Falcon 7B/40B (TII) – Trained for language generation, instruction following.

- OpenChat / OpenHermes / WizardLM – Fine-tuned models for chat and task automation.
- LM Studio – Desktop app to run LLMs locally on your PC/Mac.

Hosting Tools:

- Ollama – Easily run and switch between LLMs locally.
- LangChain + Ollama + LLaMA – Full local assistant setup.

2. Open-Source Agentic AI Frameworks

These frameworks help create autonomous or semi-autonomous AI agents for sales, research, coding, etc.

- LangChain – Framework for building agents that use tools, memory, LLMs, and databases.
- Auto-GPT – Multi-step AI agent that completes goals with minimal human input.
- AgentGPT – Web UI to create and run AI agents in-browser using open models.
- CrewAI – Task delegation to multiple cooperative agents with roles (e.g., marketer, researcher).
- SuperAGI – Full agent framework with UI, vector store, and tool integration (hugely useful for teams).
- Camel-AI – Agent-to-agent interaction platform for simulations and multi-agent tasks.

3. Open-Source Metaverse Platforms

These can be used to create virtual offices, showrooms, training spaces, or interactive team environments:

- Mozilla Hubs – Lightweight, browser-based VR spaces; ideal for meetings, events, and showcases.
- JanusXR – Web-based spatial environment creation for documents, images, and VR.
- Vircadia – Fully decentralized metaverse platform for persistent 3D worlds.
- Frame VR – Free to start, WebXR-based metaverse for meetings, events, education.
- Webaverse – Open metaverse engine for developers to build immersive apps with NFTs, avatars, and AI bots.
- OpenSimulator – Powerful engine for building large-scale virtual worlds, used in enterprise and education.

Bonus: Combine All 3

You can create a powerful, all-open tech stack:

Use LLaMA 3 or Mistral via Ollama

Add LangChain for task-driven agents

<u>Build a virtual office in Mozilla Hubs where agents assist users or customers inside the Metaverse</u>

Step-by-step guide to set up a free AI Agent inside a Metaverse room using open-source tools:

Goal:

Create a virtual room (e.g., for meetings, customer service, or demos) in the Metaverse, with an AI agent (chatbot or task assistant) integrated to interact with users.

Tools Used:

- Mozilla Hubs – Metaverse platform for virtual rooms.
- LangChain + Ollama – For running and controlling an AI agent locally.
- LLaMA 3 / Mistral – Free LLM to power the agent.
- Botpress or Rasa (optional) – To give the agent voice/chat interface.
- WebSockets / REST API – To connect the AI agent to Mozilla Hubs.

Step-by-Step Guide

Step 1: Set up Mozilla Hubs Room

Go to https://hubs.mozilla.com/

Click "Create Room"

Customize the room (name, environment)

Invite others using the room link

Use a 3D avatar to represent your AI agent (you can use a robot model)

Step 2: Run Your Own LLM Agent (Locally or on Server)

Option A: Use Ollama (Locally)

bash

CopyEdit

brew install ollama # or Windows/Linux install instructions
ollama run llama3 # or ollama run mistral

Option B: Use LangChain for Task Agents

Install LangChain and Python dependencies:

bash

pip install langchain openai streamlit

Step 3: Connect LLM Agent to Hubs

Mozilla Hubs has a Spoke API and supports JavaScript injection through custom bots.

Use Hubs Cloud Bot Sample

Connect your LangChain agent using:

WebSocket bridge from your LLM agent

JavaScript listener inside Hubs that fetches response from agent API

Example:

```
socket.onmessage = async (message) => {
const agentReply = await fetch('/get-agent-response', {
method: 'POST',
body: JSON.stringify({ userMessage: message.data })
});
speakInRoom(await agentReply.text());
};
```

Step 4: Make Agent Speak or Show Text in Hubs

- Use TTS (Text-to-Speech) like Coqui.ai to give your bot a voice
- Or show messages in 3D floating text or chat window

Step 5: (Optional) Add Personality & Tasks

Use LangGraph or CrewAI to build multiple agents (e.g., Greeter, Support, Demo bot)

Customize them with tools and memory to simulate real behavior

Demo Ideas You Can Try:

- AI receptionist in Metaverse to greet and guide visitors
- Investor pitch demo with an AI that answers startup FAQs
- Virtual showroom where the bot walks users through your products
- Support center with a bot solving user queries in real time

CHAPTER SIX

Data-Driven Decision Making with AI & Analytics

Introduction

In today's fast-paced business world, data is one of the most valuable resources available to startups. However, it's not just the collection of data that matters; it's how that data is analyzed and used to inform decisions. This chapter explores how AI-powered analytics and data-driven strategies can help startups make better, faster, and more informed decisions, leading to growth and efficiency.

6.1 Understanding Data-Driven Decision Making

Data-driven decision-making refers to the process of collecting, analyzing, and using data to guide business choices. This approach is especially crucial for startups that need to make quick, impactful decisions while operating with limited resources. By leveraging data and analytics tools, startups can:

- Identify Market Trends: Understand customer behavior, market demands, and industry shifts.
- Optimize Operations: Streamline internal processes and improve resource allocation.
- Enhance Customer Experience: Personalize marketing efforts and improve user satisfaction.
- Predict Outcomes: Use predictive analytics to forecast future trends and make proactive decisions.

6.2 The Role of AI and Machine Learning in Data Analytics

AI and Machine Learning (ML) are powerful tools that enable startups to turn raw data into actionable insights. Here's how they can help:

- Data Processing and Cleaning: AI can automate the process of cleaning large datasets, making it faster and more accurate, ensuring that startups have access to reliable information.
- Predictive Analytics: ML algorithms can analyze historical data to identify patterns and predict future outcomes, allowing startups to anticipate customer needs or market shifts.
- Personalization: AI can create personalized experiences for customers based on their preferences, purchase history, and behaviors. This can significantly enhance marketing efforts and customer retention.
- Natural Language Processing (NLP): AI-powered NLP can analyze unstructured data, such as customer feedback or social media mentions, helping startups

gain insights into customer sentiment.

6.3 Types of Analytics for Startups

Startups can leverage different types of analytics to gain deeper insights into their business operations:

Descriptive Analytics:

- Focuses on analyzing historical data to understand what happened in the past.
- Example: Analyzing sales data to determine monthly revenue trends.

Diagnostic Analytics:

- Aims to understand why something happened by identifying correlations and causes.

Example:

- Analyzing customer churn rates to determine factors contributing to retention issues.

Predictive Analytics:

- Uses historical data and statistical algorithms to forecast future outcomes.

Example:

- Predicting future sales growth based on past performance and market trends.

Prescriptive Analytics:

- Provides recommendations for actions based on data analysis.

<u>Example:</u>

- AI recommending the best time to launch a new marketing campaign to maximize ROI.

6.4 Key AI and Analytics Tools for Startups

Startups can leverage several AI and analytics tools that are both cost-effective and powerful:

Google Analytics:
A free tool to analyze web traffic and gain insights into user behavior on your website. It can help startups track key metrics like bounce rate, conversion rate, and user acquisition sources.

<u>Tableau:</u>
A popular data visualization tool that turns data into interactive, easy-to-understand dashboards. Startups can use Tableau to visualize key performance indicators (KPIs) and monitor business health.

<u>Power BI:</u>
Microsoft's data visualization tool that integrates well with other Microsoft products. It's great for small businesses looking for an affordable solution to create reports and dashboards from their data.

<u>Kissmetrics:</u>
A customer analytics platform that helps startups track customer behavior across various touchpoints and optimize marketing efforts.

<u>AI-Powered CRM Tools (e.g., HubSpot, Zoho CRM):</u>
These tools offer AI-driven insights, such as lead scoring and predictive sales forecasting, to help startups streamline

their customer relationship management processes.

DataRobot:

An automated machine learning platform that allows startups to build predictive models with minimal coding experience. It is perfect for startups that want to use AI without needing to build everything from scratch.

Hootsuite Insights (powered by Brandwatch):

An AI-driven social media monitoring tool that analyzes customer sentiment, tracks brand mentions, and gathers insights from social media data.

6.5 Building a Data Strategy for Your Startup

Startups often overlook the importance of having a solid data strategy. Here's how to develop one:

Identify Your Business Goals:

What do you want to achieve with your data? Whether it's improving customer satisfaction, increasing sales, or optimizing operations, understanding your goals is the first step in creating a data strategy.

Collect and Centralize Your Data:

Ensure that all your data (customer data, sales data, social media data, etc.) is collected and stored in a central repository. This makes it easier to analyze and make data-driven decisions.

Choose the Right Tools:

Depending on your goals, choose the appropriate tools for data collection, analysis, and visualization. For example, Google Analytics for website performance, HubSpot for CRM, and Tableau for data visualization.

Ensure Data Quality:

Data accuracy is crucial for making informed decisions. Make sure your data is clean and accurate before analyzing it. Use tools like Talend or Alteryx to automate the data-cleaning process.

<u>Implement Data Privacy and Security:</u>
With the increasing importance of data, startups must implement proper data security and privacy measures. Ensure that your business complies with data protection regulations, such as GDPR, and uses secure storage solutions.

6.6 Case Study: AI and Data Analytics in Action

Let's look at a real-world example of a startup using AI and data analytics to drive success.

<u>Company:</u> Zynga (Mobile Game Developer)

<u>Problem:</u> Zynga faced challenges in understanding player behavior and retaining users.

<u>Solution:</u>

- Zynga implemented AI algorithms to track player behavior, understand what keeps users engaged, and predict when players might stop using the app.
- By analyzing in-game data, Zynga created personalized recommendations and in-game events, which increased user engagement.
- Predictive analytics helped the company understand when to introduce new content, leading to higher retention rates and longer player lifetimes.

<u>Outcome:</u> Zynga increased its player retention by 15% and generated significant growth in revenue by using data to make informed decisions.

6.7 How AI and Analytics Enable Scalability for Startups

AI and data analytics are crucial for startups that are looking to scale. Here's how they contribute to scalability:

- Automation: As startups grow, processes that were once done manually become time-consuming. AI can automate repetitive tasks such as data collection, reporting, and even customer support, allowing startups to scale without hiring a large team.
- Improved Efficiency: AI helps optimize business operations by analyzing workflows, identifying bottlenecks, and suggesting improvements. This leads to greater operational efficiency and cost savings.
- Personalized Marketing: With AI-powered analytics, startups can create hyper-targeted marketing campaigns based on detailed customer data, allowing them to engage with customers more effectively and boost conversions.
- Scalable Customer Support: AI-powered chatbots can handle an increasing number of customer inquiries, providing instant responses and freeing up customer service teams for more complex issues.

Takeaway

Data-driven decision-making powered by AI and analytics can significantly impact a startup's ability to grow and scale. By leveraging the right tools and developing a solid data strategy, startups can make smarter decisions, enhance customer experiences, and streamline operations, all while using minimal resources.

Integrating Technologies for Modern Healthcare

In this chapter we will see the benefit of an integrating all the technologies like AI, Blockchain, IOT, Metaverse and Agentic AI for the new generation of automation solutions in the case of Pharma & Lifesciences.

The architecture is built on interconnected digital layers that power the next-gen supply chain and care delivery models. It combines real-time data collection, intelligent decision-making, secure transactions, immersive engagement, and robust governance — enabling agility, transparency, and personalization.

Let us first see the key problems that we face across the domains of Healthcare , Pharm and Life sciences.

Where Healthcare, Pharma & Life-Sciences Hurt—and How a Unified Tech Stack Can Heal Them

Modern care and drug-development still creak under decades-old workflows: data live in silos, trials limp along on paper, and supply chains remain opaque. Below is a tour of the ten pain-points that cost the industry billions and the specific combinations of AI, IoT, blockchain, metaverse spaces, digital-twins and agentic orchestration that can relieve them—right now, even on a start-up budget.

1 | Fragmented Patient Data

- **Problem.** Hospitals, labs, insurers and wearables all hold different shards of a patient's story.
- **Why it sticks.** Closed EHR vendors, privacy laws, lack of a universal ID.
- **Tech remedy.** Use IoT/FHIR gateways to stream vitals, anchor every update on a patient-owned blockchain ledger, then let an LLM "record-unifier" agent translate codes and surface one longitudinal view.

2 | Manual, Slow Clinical Trials

- **Problem.** 80 % of studies miss enrolment targets; data entry errors abound.
- **Fix.** Recruit globally in a metaverse research lounge, monitor endpoints through connected wearables, and release milestone payments automatically via smart contracts. Digital-twin "virtual cohorts" trim protocol cycles before a single patient is dosed.

3 | Counterfeits & Cold-Chain Breaches

- **Problem.** Multi-tier wholesalers mask provenance; temp excursions spoil biologics.
- **Fix.** Attach low-cost IoT sensors that publish tamper-proof temperature hashes to a permissioned blockchain. Anomaly-detection agents reroute shipments and alert regulators within minutes.

4 | Prior-Auth & Claims Gridlock

- **Problem.** Clinicians fax mountains of paperwork; approvals take weeks.
- **Fix.** An LLM agent pulls tumour genetics, guideline citations and past therapies into a structured FHIR bundle, submits via payer API, and tracks approval status—often within the same day.

5 | Alert Fatigue & Burn-out

- **Problem.** Nurses receive hundreds of low-value alarms per shift.
- **Fix.** Context-aware agents score alerts by mortality risk, suppress 70% of noise, and auto-document vitals with voice-first scribing so staff focus on patients, not keyboards.

6 | Poor Medication Adherence

- **Problem.** Forgetfulness, cost pressures, lack of feedback loops.
- **Fix.** Smart-pill bottles stream usage; when doses are missed, an avatar coach appears on the patient's phone, explains consequences, and issues token incentives redeemable for refills.

7 | Drug-Discovery Bottlenecks

- **Problem.** Wet-lab iterations are slow and costly.

- **Fix.** Generative-AI models design candidate molecules; cloud-based digital-twin cells run in-silico assays to predict toxicity; only the top 1 % move to physical synthesis, shaving years off R-and-D.

8 | Episodic, Non-Personalised Care

- **Problem.** Health systems pay for procedures, not outcomes.
- **Fix.** Edge-AI wearables analyse ECG locally; an agent schedules video check-ins, while a metaverse rehab gym gamifies therapy sessions, all wrapped in value-based smart-contract payments.

9 | Privacy & Algorithmic Bias

Problem. PHI breaches erode trust; opaque models risk discrimination.
Fix. Federated learning keeps data on-premise, homomorphic encryption secures queries, and every AI inference is logged to an immutable audit chain. Explainability wrappers show clinicians why the model fired.

10 | Training & Knowledge Decay

- **Problem.** New devices outpace staff education.
- **Fix.** Low-cost VR tutorials let nurses practise dialysis or intubation anytime; an LLM tutor agent answers SOP questions on demand, scoring competence until

mastery.

Solution Elements from the Integrated Architecture

Modern Healthcare System: A Technology-Driven Shift

An advanced healthcare system today is defined by predictive care, precision treatment, traceable operations, secure infrastructure, and immersive patient and workforce engagement. Each enabling technology plays a unique and complementary role:1. IoT – The Nervous System of Smart Healthcare

How It Helps:

- Connects medical devices, wearablesd equipment.
- Streams real-time patient vitals, asset tracking, and environmental conditions.

Impact:

- Healthcare: Remote patient monitoring, ICU alerts, ambulance telemetry.
- Pharma: Cold-chain monitoring for vaccines and biologics.
- Life Sciences: Live monitoring of clinical trial environments.

2. Artificial Intelligence – The Brain Behind Decisions

How It Helps:

- Automates diagnostics, recommends treatments, and predicts outcomes.
- AI agents can autonomously handle supply, clinical triage, or drug analysis.

Impact:

- Healthcare: AI-based triage, image diagnostics (X-ray, MRI), virtual nursing assistants.
- Pharma: Accelerated drug discovery and adverse effect prediction.
- Life Sciences: Pattern analysis in genomics and protein structure prediction.

3. Data Analytics – Turning Information into Intelligence

How It Helps:

- Extracts actionable insights from structured and unstructured data.
- Enables predictive and preventive models.

Impact:

- Healthcare: Population health analytics, hospital resource forecasting.
- Pharma: Market intelligence for formulation and distribution planning.
- Life Sciences: Patient stratification and trial outcome prediction.

<u>**4. Cloud Computing – Scalable Infrastructure for Modern Care**</u>

How It Helps

- Stores and processes large volumes of medical and operational data.
- Enables interoperability and collaboration across geographies.

Impact:

- Healthcare: Electronic Health Record (EHR) integration across hospitals.
- Pharma: Cloud labs for global R&D collaboration.
- Life Sciences: Real-time trial monitoring and decentralized research.

<u>**5. Cybersecurity – The Immune System of Digital Health**</u>

How It Helps:

- Protects sensitive data and systems from breaches and ransomware.
- Enables secure access, identity management, and compliance.

Impact:

- Healthcare: Safeguards patient data and ensures HIPAA/HiTrust compliance.

- Pharma: Secures intellectual property and research data.
- Life Sciences: Ensures ethical data access and usage during trials.

6. Metaverse – The Human Experience Layer

How It Helps:

- Creates immersive 3D environments for education, therapy, and collaboration.
- Enables realistic virtual simulations and interactions.

Impact:

- Healthcare: Remote therapy, immersive surgery prep, pain management.
- Pharma: Virtual walkthroughs of manufacturing and supply chain.
- Life Sciences: VR labs and collaborative trial design across continents.

Integrated Automation Architecture in Healthcare

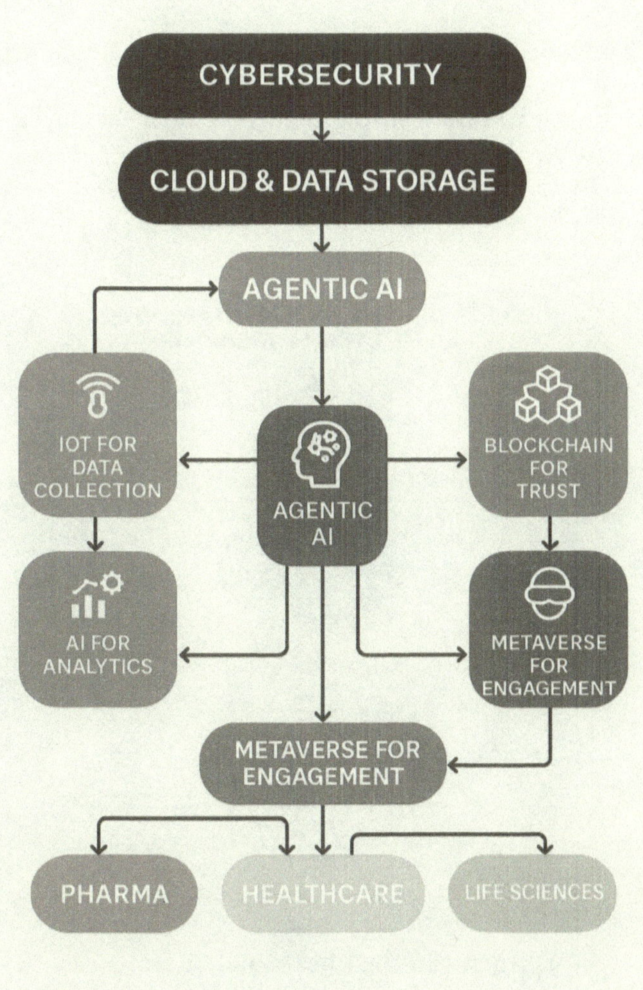

Interplay of all Technologies in Pharma healthcare & Lifesciences

The Role of AI Agents in Healthcare and Lifesciences

Some of the diffetent AI Agents that can be deployed in the Pharma, Healthcare and Lifsciences domain are depicted in the following figure.

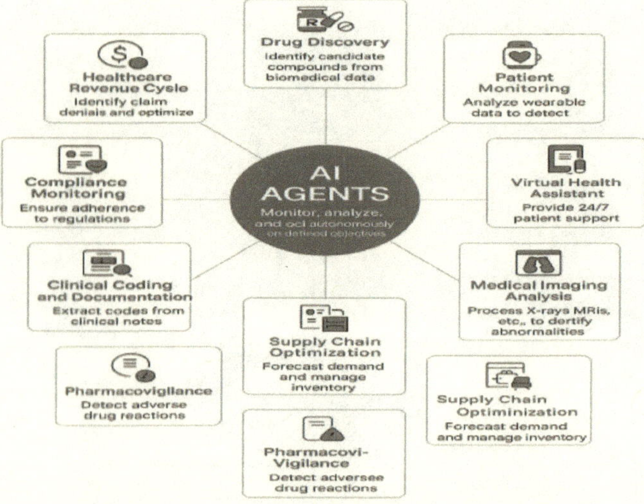

AI Agents in Healthcare and Lifesciences

The Power of Integration

This framework isn't just about technology—it's about building resilient, responsive, and intelligent systems in Pharma, Healthcare, and Life Sciences. Together, IoT, AI, Blockchain, and Metaverse form a smart and secure digital supply chain and care delivery model—one that is more human-centered, transparent, and efficient.

The future outlook for the adoption of various technologies:

Healthcare is moving from episodic, paper-centred care to a continuous, data-centric, software-defined ecosystem. The journey unfolds in four overlapping waves, each enabled by a maturing stack of AI, IoT, cloud, blockchain and immersive-tech capabilities.

Digitalisation Roadmap—From Sick-Care to Smart-Care, Lab Bench to Loading Dock

Digital transformation is no longer limited to clinic walls; it now stretches across manufacturing suites, distribution lanes, and last-mile patient touchpoints. When IoT, AI, blockchain, and immersive tech are woven into a single fabric, they create a resilient, responsive, and intelligent value chain for Pharma, Healthcare, and Life-Sciences—one that is simultaneously more human-centred and operationally lean.

1 | Data Liquidity Across Plant + Patient

Interoperable FHIR + OPC-UA streams let bioreactors, packaging lines, and EHR systems publish to the same lakehouse.

Patient-controlled wallets and device digital twins ensure that a temperature blip on a filling line is traceable all the way to an injection site.

Outcome: seamless hand-off from "batch record" to "health record."

2 | Edge-to-Cloud Intelligence in Production & Care

Edge AI on vision cameras catches vial defects in milliseconds; the same cloud platform predicts a COPD flare from a home spirometer.

Unified digital-twin dashboards let quality engineers and clinicians view the live status of every lot and every lung.

Outcome: fewer recalls, fewer readmissions.

3 | Agentic Workflow Automation

LLM super-agents auto-draft deviation reports, reconcile lot genealogy, and file prior-authorisations—shrinking cycle times on both factory floor and revenue cycle.

Smart contracts trigger supplier payments when sensors confirm cold-chain integrity, and trigger payer reimbursements when patient biomarkers hit targets.

Outcome: cash flows faster, humans focus on high-value science and care.

4 | Immersive, Distributed Collaboration

AR work-instructions guide technicians through aseptic setups; metaverse clean-room twins let regulators audit remotely.

VR rehab gyms and virtual product-launch expos extend the same immersive toolset to patients and HCPs.

Outcome: expertise travels instantly, carbon footprint shrinks.

Strategic Priorities for Stakeholders

Stakeholder	2025 Action Steps	Long-Term Wins
Start-ups	Build micro-solutions that plug into existing FHIR or claims APIs; prove ROI on one metric (e.g., readmission reduction).	Become indispensable modules in larger hospital tech-stacks.
Health Systems	Invest in unified data lakes and sandbox environments for external innovators.	Transition from fee-for-service to value-based, data-certified networks.
Payers	Pilot smart-contract reimbursement for remote monitoring devices.	Slash admin overhead and attract members with frictionless claims.
Regulators	Issue dynamic guidelines for federated learning, explainable AI and XR safety.	Foster innovation while protecting privacy and equity.
Clinicians	Upskill in AI literacy and virtual-care etiquette; co-design agent interfaces.	Regain patient-facing time and reduce burnout.

Strategic Prioriots for Stakeholders in PHLS domain

Risks to Manage

- Algorithmic bias — mandate continuous audit trails and representative training data.
- Cybersecurity — zero-trust architectures and quantum-safe encryption for IoMT.
- Digital divide — subsidise devices and connectivity for underserved populations.
- Clinician trust — pair every autonomous agent with clear explainability and override options.

By 2030, digitalised healthcare will mean a stitched-together fabric where data moves at the speed of consent, AI agents shoulder routine workloads, and immersive interfaces collapse distance between expertise and need. The winners will be organisations that treat digital not as an IT project but as the operating system of care—secure, ethical and relentlessly patient-centred

The integrated architecture is not just about technology — it's about redefining trust, speed, accuracy, and care in life-saving domains. With each layer playing a strategic role, the future of intelligent, ethical, and resilient healthcare supply chains is within reach.

CHAPTER SEVEN

Scaling Through Innovation and AI-Driven Product Development

Introduction

Scaling a startup isn't just about growing revenue or increasing market share. It's about continually evolving, innovating, and delivering value to customers at a larger scale. For many startups, product innovation is the cornerstone of growth. Artificial Intelligence (AI) is playing a pivotal role in product development and innovation, enabling startups to create smarter, more efficient, and more personalized products.

In this chapter, we will dive into how startups can use AI to enhance their product development processes, drive innovation, and scale efficiently. From automating product design to personalized product recommendations, AI offers immense potential for startups to stay competitive and meet the demands of a growing customer base.

7.1 The Role of AI in Product Innovation

Innovation is crucial for any startup looking to scale. However, innovation doesn't just come from creativity alone—it comes from utilizing the right tools and technologies to bring new ideas to life. AI accelerates product development by providing insights from data, automating routine tasks, and even suggesting improvements based on customer feedback and behavioral data.

Key ways AI drives product innovation include:

- Predictive Analytics: AI can predict trends and consumer needs, helping startups stay ahead of the curve.
- Design Automation: AI tools like Generative Design use algorithms to create innovative designs based on a set of input parameters, streamlining product development.
- Customer Insights: AI analyzes customer behavior, reviews, and feedback to identify unmet needs and areas for improvement.
- Personalization: AI enables startups to tailor products or services to individual customer preferences, enhancing customer satisfaction.

7.2 AI-Powered Product Development Processes

Startups can leverage AI throughout the entire product development lifecycle. From initial concept to final rollout,

AI can optimize each stage, reduce time to market, and ensure the final product is tailored to the needs of its customers.

<u>1. Ideation and Concept Validation</u>

Market Trend Analysis: AI can analyze large datasets to identify emerging trends, competitor products, and market gaps. Tools like Google Trends and Statista can help in assessing what customers are looking for.

Customer Sentiment Analysis: AI algorithms can analyze social media platforms, customer reviews, and forums to gauge public sentiment toward existing products, helping startups refine their ideas before development.

<u>2. Design and Prototyping</u>

Generative Design: AI-powered design tools, like Autodesk and Fusion 360, use machine learning algorithms to generate a wide range of design options based on specific requirements, such as material strength, weight, and cost. This allows for innovative product designs that may not have been conceived through traditional methods.

Simulation Tools: AI-powered simulation software can test product prototypes in virtual environments, ensuring that designs are functional and cost-effective before production begins.

<u>3. Development and Testing</u>

Automated Coding: AI-driven tools like GitHub Copilot and Tabnine assist developers by suggesting code snippets, identifying bugs, and providing solutions in real-time, accelerating the development process.

AI in QA Testing: AI tools like Test.ai automate the testing of products and software to identify bugs, performance issues, and user experience flaws, reducing the testing cycle and ensuring higher-quality products.

<u>4. Personalization and Customization</u>

AI-Driven Personalization: AI algorithms can track individual customer preferences, browsing behaviors, and interactions with the product. This data can be used to provide personalized recommendations, content, or product features. For instance, Amazon and Netflix use AI to recommend products and media based on user history.

Real-Time Feedback: AI tools can monitor user interactions with a product in real-time and suggest dynamic changes or improvements. This data-driven approach allows startups to continuously improve their product based on actual user behavior.

7.3 Case Studies: AI-Driven Product Innovation

<u>Case Study 1: Spotify</u>

Challenge: Spotify wanted to scale its service globally while maintaining a personalized user experience.

Solution: Spotify leveraged AI to offer personalized playlists, discover new artists based on listening habits, and curate content based on user preferences.

Outcome: Spotify's AI algorithms are a core part of their product innovation, driving engagement and user retention. The company's recommendation engine has played a key role in its global expansion, enabling Spotify to deliver a highly customized experience to millions of users.

<u>Case Study 2: Tesla</u>

Challenge: Tesla wanted to enhance the functionality of their electric vehicles and improve user safety.

Solution: Tesla used AI to power their Autopilot feature, which provides autonomous driving capabilities. Additionally, AI-driven software updates are regularly pushed to vehicles, enhancing performance and introducing new features.

Outcome: Tesla's AI-driven product innovation has positioned it as a leader in the electric vehicle market, with a significant competitive edge through the continual improvement of product features based on real-world data.

7.4 AI Tools for Enhancing Product Development

Startups looking to incorporate AI into their product development processes can leverage a variety of tools to streamline operations and enhance creativity. Here are some examples of AI tools that can aid in different stages of product development:

- Sketch2Code: A Microsoft AI tool that converts hand-drawn designs into HTML code, helping designers quickly prototype and iterate on web-based products.
- H2O.ai: An open-source AI platform that provides machine learning capabilities for data analysis, predictive modeling, and real-time decision-making, assisting in product ideation and feature enhancements.
- DeepAI: A suite of AI tools for image processing, text generation, and language understanding, which can be used in various product design aspects, such as automated content generation and personalization.
- ChatGPT: Startups can use ChatGPT for ideation, creating content, writing product descriptions, generating responses for chatbots, and more.
- TensorFlow: An open-source machine learning library that enables startups to build AI models for predictive analytics, user behavior analysis, and more.
- AutoML: Tools like Google Cloud AutoML and DataRobot provide automated machine learning capabilities for startups to develop custom AI models without the need for advanced data science expertise.

7.5 Leveraging AI for Product Iteration and Scaling

Once a product is launched, AI can continue to play a pivotal role in its evolution and scaling. As startups grow and face the challenge of serving a larger customer base, AI provides insights and solutions to help scale effectively.

<u>1. Product Iteration</u>

AI can analyze customer feedback and identify areas for improvement, allowing for rapid product iterations.

Startups can use AI-driven analytics to measure how users interact with the product, which features are most used, and which aspects need refinement.

<u>2. Scaling Customer Personalization</u>

As a startup's user base expands, AI ensures that personalization doesn't get lost. AI can segment customers based on behaviors, demographics, and purchase patterns, ensuring that each customer receives tailored experiences as the product scales.

<u>3. Predictive Scaling</u>

AI can predict when a product will hit a scalability bottleneck, whether it's server load, customer support capacity, or product feature performance. By identifying these bottlenecks early, startups can scale proactively and avoid issues that could harm customer experience.

7.6 Best Practices for AI-Powered Product Development

When integrating AI into product development, startups should follow these best practices to maximize its effectiveness:

- Start with Data: Data is the foundation of AI. Ensure that your product has access to high-quality, structured data to make AI applications more effective.
- Iterate Based on Feedback: Use AI-driven insights to make iterative changes to the product based on user

feedback and real-time data.

- Ensure Data Privacy: When using AI to personalize products or analyze user data, ensure that you comply with data privacy regulations like GDPR and CCPA to protect user trust.
- Experiment and Test: Don't be afraid to test new ideas using AI. A/B testing and rapid prototyping using AI can help uncover breakthrough innovations quickly.
- Leverage Open-Source Tools: Open-source AI tools and frameworks offer startups access to powerful AI capabilities without the need for extensive investment in proprietary systems.

7.7 The Future of AI in Product Innovation

As AI technologies continue to evolve, the future of product development will become increasingly driven by automation, machine learning, and deep data insights. Startups will have the ability to create smarter, more intuitive products that are personalized for every user. AI will enable not just the creation of new products but also the constant enhancement and refinement of existing ones.

The future of product innovation lies in the ability to integrate AI seamlessly into the development process, allowing startups to stay nimble, scalable, and ahead of the competition.

Takeaway

AI is not just a tool for product development—it is a catalyst for innovation, personalization, and scalability. By incorporating AI into their product development lifecycle, startups can accelerate the creation of cutting-edge products, stay competitive, and offer enhanced experiences to their customers. As startups scale, AI will continue to be a driving force in enabling them to meet growing demands and continuously improve their offerings.

CHAPTER EIGHT

Automating Operations with AI

Introduction

Startups are often resource-constrained, which means they need to be highly efficient in every aspect of their operations. One of the most effective ways to achieve this is through automation. In this chapter, we will explore how Artificial Intelligence (AI) can help startups automate repetitive tasks, optimize workflows, and scale their operations without increasing headcount.

8.1 The Importance of Automation for Startups

Automation plays a vital role in helping startups save time, reduce operational costs, and improve consistency. By automating mundane, repetitive tasks, startups can focus on core activities like strategy development, innovation, and customer acquisition.

Key benefits of automation for startups include:

- Improved Efficiency: Automation streamlines business processes, making them faster and more accurate.
- Cost Reduction: By automating tasks that would otherwise require manual effort, startups can reduce their operational costs and allocate resources more effectively.
- Scalability: Automation allows startups to handle increased demand without needing to significantly increase staff or resources.
- Consistency: Automated processes eliminate the human error factor, ensuring that tasks are executed consistently and at a high level of accuracy.

8.2 Key Areas of Automation for Startups

AI can automate a wide range of processes across different areas of a startup's operations. Some of the key areas to consider automating are:

1. Customer Support

Chatbots: AI-powered chatbots can handle common customer inquiries, provide support, and guide customers through troubleshooting processes. This reduces the workload of customer service teams, allowing them to focus on more complex issues.

AI-driven Help Desks: AI can categorize and route customer queries to the appropriate support agents, ensuring faster response times and better customer satisfaction.

2. Marketing

Email Marketing Automation: AI can analyze customer data and segment audiences for more targeted email campaigns. It can also personalize emails, send them at the optimal times, and track campaign performance.

Social Media Scheduling and Engagement: Tools like Hootsuite or Buffer use AI to schedule posts, track engagement, and suggest optimal posting times based on user activity.

Customer Journey Automation: AI-driven platforms can create personalized marketing journeys for individual customers, guiding them through every stage of the funnel based on their behavior and interactions with your brand.

3. Sales and Lead Management

Lead Scoring: AI tools like HubSpot and Salesforce use machine learning algorithms to automatically score leads based on their engagement and likelihood of conversion. This allows sales teams to prioritize high-potential leads.

Automated Sales Outreach: AI can send personalized follow-up emails, schedule meetings, and even make initial contact with prospects, reducing the workload of the sales team.

CRM Automation: AI can automatically update and manage customer records, ensuring that your CRM system stays up-to-date and accurate.

4. Inventory Management

Smart Inventory Systems: AI-powered inventory management systems can forecast demand, track stock levels, and place automatic orders to suppliers when inventory is low. This minimizes the risk of stockouts and overstocking.

Automated Supply Chain Optimization: AI can optimize routes for deliveries and suggest inventory replenishment strategies, making your supply chain more efficient and cost-effective.

5. Accounting and Finance

Automated Invoicing: AI can generate and send invoices automatically based on predefined criteria, saving time and reducing errors.

Expense Management: AI tools can track expenses, categorize them, and even flag any unusual or unnecessary costs. This helps startups stay on top of their financial health.

AI-Powered Financial Forecasting: By analyzing historical financial data, AI can help predict future revenue, expenses, and cash flow, enabling startups to make more informed financial decisions.

8.3 AI Tools for Automating Startup Operations

There are a variety of AI tools available that can help startups automate various aspects of their operations:

- Zapier: A tool that connects apps and automates workflows, such as triggering actions based on certain events (e.g., automatically creating tasks in Trello when a new lead enters your CRM).
- Chatfuel: A platform for building AI-powered chatbots that can handle customer inquiries, process orders, and engage users on messaging platforms like Facebook Messenger.
- Intercom: An AI-powered customer support platform that automates messaging and provides live chat services to engage customers.
- HubSpot CRM: A tool for managing leads, automating follow-up emails, and managing sales workflows. Its AI features help with lead scoring and pipeline management.
- Xero: An accounting tool that automates invoicing, expense tracking, and financial reporting, saving startups valuable time.
- Airtable: A flexible project management tool that automates processes like data entry, task assignments,

and notifications across your team.

8.4 How Automation Can Enable Scalability

One of the biggest challenges for startups is scaling their operations as they grow. Automation makes it possible to scale effectively without having to hire a large number of additional employees. Here's how automation facilitates scalability:

- Faster Onboarding: With automated systems in place, you can onboard new employees, clients, and customers quickly and efficiently.
- Improved Resource Allocation: By automating time-consuming tasks, startups can free up human resources to focus on higher-value activities, such as business development or strategic planning.
- Consistency Across Operations: Automation ensures that processes remain consistent as the business grows, reducing the likelihood of errors and ensuring a high-quality experience for customers.
- Scalable Customer Support: AI-driven chatbots can handle an increasing volume of customer inquiries, enabling startups to provide support to a growing customer base without expanding the support team.

8.5 Case Study: How AI Automation Helped a Startup Scale

Company: FreshBooks (Cloud-Based Accounting Software)

Challenge: FreshBooks, a small startup offering accounting software, needed to scale its operations without dramatically increasing overhead costs.

Solution:

- FreshBooks implemented AI-driven tools to automate invoicing, payments, and customer support.
- They also automated customer onboarding processes, reducing the time and effort needed to integrate new customers into the system.
- AI-powered chatbots and customer service platforms helped manage customer inquiries and reduce the workload on their support team.

Outcome:

- FreshBooks scaled to a global customer base with minimal increase in staff.
- Automated invoicing and payment processing resulted in a significant reduction in administrative costs.
- The company saw increased customer satisfaction due to faster response times and a seamless user experience.

8.6 Best Practices for Implementing Automation in Your Startup

While automation offers significant benefits, it's important to approach it strategically. Here are some best practices for implementing automation in your startup:

- Start Small and Scale Gradually: Begin by automating simple, low-risk tasks before scaling up to more complex processes.
- Choose the Right Tools: Research and choose the tools that best fit your startup's needs. Focus on tools that integrate well with your existing systems.
- Monitor and Optimize: After implementing automation, monitor its effectiveness regularly and make adjustments as needed to improve performance.

- Maintain a Human Touch: While automation is helpful, there are still many aspects of customer interaction that require a human touch. Use automation to handle repetitive tasks, but ensure that your team is available for complex customer issues.

8.7 The Future of Automation in Startups

As technology continues to evolve, the scope of automation in startups will only grow. The future of automation is headed toward more advanced AI systems capable of handling complex decision-making processes, deep learning, and even predictive analytics to improve business outcomes.

The possibilities for startups to automate their operations are endless, from AI-driven decision support systems to fully automated workflows. Embracing these advancements will help startups stay ahead of the competition and thrive in a rapidly changing business environment.

Takeaway

AI-driven automation is a game-changer for startups, allowing them to streamline operations, reduce costs, and scale efficiently. By automating tasks across various business functions such as marketing, customer support, sales, and accounting, startups can focus their limited resources on what truly matters: innovation and growth.

Digitalisation of Manufacturing

In this chapter we will see the case study of an integrated AI, IOT, Blockchain and Data analytics platforms to Digitalise Manufacturing offering high productivity and profitability.

Integrated MohSoft AI & Mobillor Smart Manufacturing Platform

Concept Overview

MohSoft and Mobillor are joining forces to create an integrated Digitalization & Digital Transformation platform for manufacturing plants. This next-generation solution leverages process digitization, Distributed Ledger Technology (DLT), and Business Analytics to enhance operational efficiency, transparency, and real-time decision-making in manufacturing.

The platform integrates AI-driven analytics, IoT, DLT, and automation to provide manufacturers with end-to-end visibility, predictive insights, and secure, tamper-proof transactions across supply chains, production lines, and distribution networks.

Problem Statement in most of the manufacturing industries across sectors is captured as follows in the form of challenges faced.

Challenges in Traditional Manufacturing

Manufacturers face several inefficiencies and operational bottlenecks, including:

- Siloed & Manual Processes – Lack of real-time integration between supply chain, production, maintenance, and distribution.
- Lack of Data Visibility – No single source of truth, leading to delays in decision-making.
- High Maintenance Costs – Reactive rather than predictive maintenance leads to costly downtime.
- Supply Chain Disruptions – Poor supplier collaboration, delayed shipments, and misaligned procurement.
- Quality & Compliance Issues – Inability to track defects, regulatory non-compliance, and counterfeit risks.
- Inefficient Distribution & Demand Forecasting – Fragmented distribution networks result in stockouts or excess inventory.

These challenges lead to low productivity, operational inefficiencies, and revenue loss, necessitating a fully integrated digital transformation solution.

Solution: MohSoft & Mobillor Smart Manufacturing Platform

The following figure depicts the end to end digitisation of processes in a manufacturing plant and implementation of advanced Data analytics & Distributed Ledger Technologies to arrive at actionable insights.

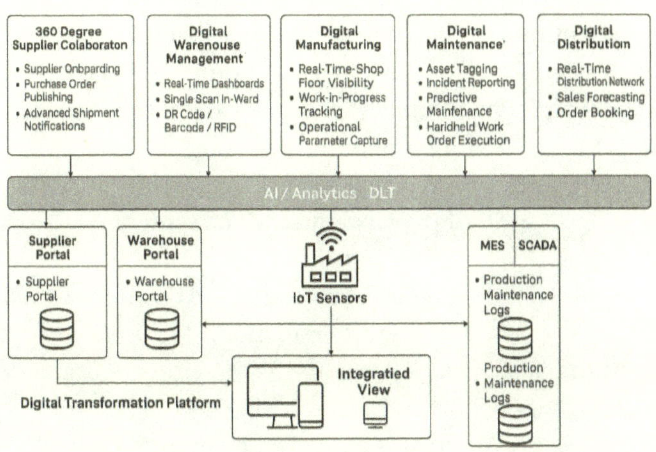

Enter Integrated Smart Manufacturing Automation platform

Integrated Smart Manufacturing Automation Courtesy Mohsoft Technologies and Mobillor Technolgies.

The integrated AI-powered, DLT-enabled digital transformation platform addresses manufacturing inefficiencies by providing:

1. 360° Supplier Collaboration

- Seamless Supplier Onboarding – AI-driven supplier verification and onboarding.
- Real-time Order Management – DLT-powered smart purchase orders with real-time status tracking.
- Supply Chain Visibility – Automated Advanced Shipment Notifications (ASN) and tamper-proof transaction records using DLT.

2. Digital Warehouse Management

- Real-Time Inventory Dashboards – AI-powered stock-level prediction.
- Automated Inward Process – Single-scan QR/barcode/RFID tracking.
- Smart Auditing – AI-driven inventory audits & reconciliation with ERP integration.

3. Digital Manufacturing

- Shop Floor Intelligence – Real-time production monitoring via IoT sensors & AI.
- Work-in-Progress (WIP) Tracking – End-to-end traceability of manufacturing processes.
- Operational Parameter Capture – MES/SCADA integration for real-time machine performance tracking.

4. Digital Maintenance

- AI-Driven Predictive Maintenance – Preventive analytics for machine health.
- Asset Tagging & Incident Reporting – DLT-powered maintenance history tracking.
- Work Order Management – Handheld-enabled mobile execution of maintenance tasks.

5. Digital Distribution & Analytics

- Real-Time Distribution Network Visibility – AI-driven logistics optimization.
- Sales Forecasting & Order Booking – Predictive analytics for demand planning.
- End-to-End Traceability – Blockchain-powered secure tracking of product movements.

Key Applications of the Integrated Platform

1. Smart Manufacturing Plants

- Real-time shop floor monitoring.
- AI-driven defect detection & process optimization.

2. Automotive Industry

- Predictive maintenance for assembly lines.
- AI-based production planning & quality control.

3. Pharmaceutical & Healthcare Manufacturing

- Blockchain-based drug traceability & compliance.

- AI-powered demand forecasting for raw materials.

4. Aerospace & Defense

- Secure supplier collaboration with immutable records.
- AI-driven defect tracking & maintenance.

5. Consumer Electronics & Appliances

- Intelligent inventory tracking for parts & components.
- AI-powered sales forecasting for distribution efficiency.

6. Oil & Gas / Heavy Machinery

- Digital twins for real-time asset monitoring.
- Predictive failure analysis for expensive equipment.

Conclusion

The MohSoft AI & Mobillor Smart Manufacturing Platform provides an end-to-end digital transformation solution by integrating AI, IoT, DLT, and analytics. It enables real-time visibility, process automation, predictive insights, and secure transactions, making it the ultimate solution for Industry 4.0 enterprises looking to achieve higher efficiency, lower costs, and enhanced security.

CHAPTER NINE

Growing Your Startup with AI-Driven Marketing and Sales

Introduction

Marketing and sales are the driving forces behind any startup's growth. As a startup scales, traditional methods of marketing and sales may not be sufficient to reach the target audience effectively or efficiently. To thrive in a competitive landscape, startups must leverage AI to optimize their marketing and sales processes. AI can help startups enhance customer targeting, improve engagement, automate processes, and drive conversions with higher precision.

In this chapter, we will explore how startups can harness AI to transform their marketing and sales strategies. From hyper-targeted campaigns to predictive analytics, AI provides an array of tools that allow businesses to operate smarter, not harder.

9.1 The Power of AI in Marketing

Marketing has become more data-driven and personalized than ever before. AI allows startups to gain deeper insights into customer behavior, preferences, and trends, enabling them to deliver tailored marketing campaigns that resonate with the target audience.

<u>1. Customer Segmentation</u>

- AI-Powered Customer Segmentation: Traditional customer segmentation is often based on broad demographic information. With AI, startups can create hyper-targeted segments based on behavioral data, buying patterns, and even psychographics. Tools like HubSpot and Segment use machine learning algorithms to segment customers dynamically and enable startups to serve personalized content, offers, and communications to each group.
- Behavioral Insights: AI can help analyze past customer behavior to identify patterns and trends, which can be used to forecast future purchasing behavior.

<u>2. Personalized Marketing Campaigns</u>

- Email Campaigns: AI can be used to tailor email campaigns to individual customers by analyzing their past interactions, preferences, and buying behaviors. For example, Mailchimp and SendGrid offer AI-powered email automation tools that personalize subject lines, content, and send times based on individual user behavior.

- Dynamic Content: AI-driven content platforms such as Dynamic Yield enable startups to create dynamic landing pages or ads that change based on customer preferences or behaviors.

3. Chatbots and Conversational Marketing

- AI Chatbots: Conversational AI can help startups engage customers in real-time, answer their queries, and even close sales. Platforms like Drift, Intercom, and Tidio use AI to enable real-time customer interaction, providing immediate responses to customer inquiries and guiding them through the sales funnel.
- Conversational Funnels: AI chatbots can collect and analyze customer data during conversations, qualifying leads and directing them to the appropriate sales representatives, significantly improving lead conversion rates.

4. Predictive Analytics for Campaign Performance

- Predicting Campaign Outcomes: AI-driven tools like Google Analytics and Hootsuite Insights can predict the success of marketing campaigns based on historical data and real-time analytics. These insights help startups allocate marketing resources more efficiently, optimizing campaigns for maximum return on investment.
- A/B Testing Automation: AI can run A/B tests on various marketing strategies (ad copy, creatives, target demographics) and automatically adjust campaigns to maximize performance.

9.2 AI in Sales Process Automation

Sales is an essential part of any business, but as a startup scales, managing the sales process manually becomes increasingly challenging. AI can help automate repetitive tasks, forecast sales performance, and improve lead qualification, allowing sales teams to focus on high-value activities.

<u>1. Lead Generation and Qualification</u>

- Automated Lead Scoring: AI can automatically score leads based on behavior and demographic data, ensuring that sales teams focus on the most promising prospects. Tools like HubSpot and Salesforce Einstein use AI to qualify leads by analyzing their likelihood to convert.
- Lead Generation Chatbots: AI chatbots can also help generate leads by interacting with visitors on the website, qualifying them based on predefined criteria, and pushing qualified leads into the CRM system.

<u>2. Sales Forecasting</u>

- Predictive Sales Analytics: AI-driven tools like Clari and Zia (from Zoho CRM) use machine learning algorithms to analyze historical sales data, providing accurate sales forecasts and suggesting the most effective strategies for meeting sales goals.
- Pipeline Management: AI can help identify bottlenecks in the sales pipeline, allowing sales managers to take corrective actions before issues escalate. By analyzing historical performance, AI also helps identify the best times to reach out to prospects, increasing the likelihood of successful conversions.

3. Customer Relationship Management (CRM)

- AI-Enhanced CRM: CRMs like Salesforce Einstein use AI to analyze customer data and provide actionable insights, including identifying cross-sell or up-sell opportunities, tracking customer sentiment, and predicting future behaviors. This helps sales teams build stronger relationships with customers and improve retention rates.
- Automated Follow-ups: AI can automate follow-up messages and reminders based on customer interactions, ensuring that no opportunity is missed.

9.3 AI Tools for Marketing and Sales Success

Here are some essential AI tools that startups can use to enhance their marketing and sales strategies:

- HubSpot: Offers AI-powered marketing automation tools, including email marketing, content management, and lead scoring.
- Drift: A conversational marketing platform that uses AI chatbots to engage customers, qualify leads, and accelerate sales.
- Salesforce Einstein: AI-powered CRM tool that provides predictive analytics, lead scoring, and sales forecasting.
- Google Analytics: Uses AI and machine learning to track and predict website visitor behavior, providing insights that optimize marketing strategies.
- Mailchimp: AI-powered email marketing automation that personalizes email content and sends based on customer behavior.
- Hootsuite Insights: An AI tool for social media marketing, providing analytics and predictive insights

into audience behavior and engagement.

- PandaDoc: A document automation tool that leverages AI to help sales teams create, track, and close deals more efficiently.

9.4 AI-Powered Social Media Marketing

Social media is one of the most effective ways for startups to engage with their audience and build brand recognition. AI-driven tools can help businesses optimize their social media presence and measure the effectiveness of their campaigns.

<u>1. Content Creation and Curation</u>

- AI Content Generators: Tools like Copy.ai and Jasper use natural language processing (NLP) to generate creative content for blogs, social media posts, and advertisements.
- Content Curation: AI tools can help curate content by analyzing customer preferences and delivering relevant content that resonates with the target audience. Platforms like Curata use AI to discover trending topics and share content based on user interests.

<u>2. Social Media Insights</u>

- AI Social Listening: AI tools such as Brandwatch and Sprout Social monitor social media conversations in real-time, identifying trends and customer sentiments. This data can help startups create more relevant content, improve customer engagement, and respond to customer feedback.
- Sentiment Analysis: AI can analyze customer sentiment toward a brand or product by examining social media

posts, reviews, and comments. Tools like MonkeyLearn provide sentiment analysis features that allow businesses to gauge public perception and adjust their marketing strategies accordingly.

3. Automated Social Media Scheduling

- AI-Driven Scheduling: Platforms like Buffer and Later use AI to optimize social media post scheduling by analyzing when the audience is most active, ensuring maximum reach and engagement.

9.5 Best Practices for Implementing AI in Marketing and Sales

While AI offers numerous benefits, there are certain best practices that startups should follow to ensure they're using AI effectively in their marketing and sales strategies:

- Start Small and Scale Gradually: Begin by incorporating AI in small, manageable aspects of marketing and sales. Test tools and strategies on a small scale, measure success, and then expand.
- Focus on Data Quality: AI is only as good as the data it receives. Ensure that you have clean, organized, and up-to-date data before using AI tools.
- Continuous Optimization: AI tools continuously learn and improve over time. Regularly analyze the performance of AI-driven campaigns and refine strategies based on insights.
- Human-AI Collaboration: AI should augment the efforts of your marketing and sales teams, not replace them. Use AI for automation and insights, but allow your team to focus on creativity and relationship-building.

- Experiment with A/B Testing: Use AI-driven A/B testing tools to find the most effective strategies and continuously optimize your marketing and sales approach.

9.6 The Future of AI in Marketing and Sales

The future of AI in marketing and sales is undoubtedly bright. As AI technologies continue to evolve, startups will have even more powerful tools at their disposal to target, engage, and convert customers. The future of marketing and sales will be increasingly automated, personalized, and data-driven, with AI playing a central role in every aspect of the process.

9.7 Agentic AI Based approach to Sales and Marketing

Here's an Agentic AI-based approach for implementing the Integrated AI-Based Marketing System, transforming the traditional automation model into a multi-agent ecosystem with modular intelligence and coordination across customer journey stages.

Agentic AI for sales and Marketing: Integrated approach

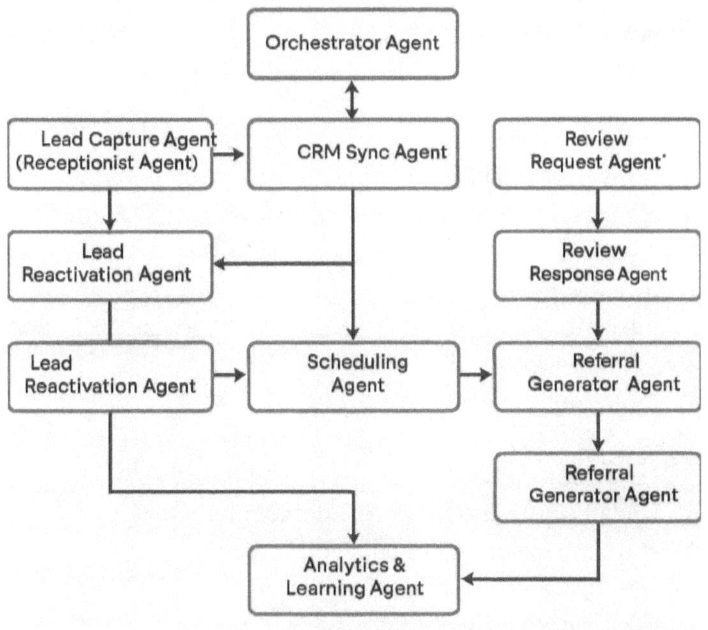

Agentic AI-Based Marketing System: Modular Agent Architecture

Overview:

Instead of a monolithic automation platform, this model employs specialized AI agents—each with distinct roles—coordinated through a central orchestrator. These agents communicate, share data, and act based on goals, triggers, and policies to autonomously handle marketing operations.

Core Agents & Their Roles

i) Lead Capture Agent (Receptionist Agent)
Purpose: Greet and interact with inbound visitors via chat, voice, or forms.
Functions:

- Initial qualification (intent, budget, urgency)
- Conversational lead nurturing
- Handoff to CRM and other agents

ii) CRM Sync Agent
Purpose: Ensure real-time data sync across CRM and lead databases.
Functions:

- Fetch historic lead lists
- Update status based on AI interactions
- Maintain clean, enriched lead profiles

iii) Lead Reactivation Agent
Purpose: Re-engage dormant or cold leads.
Functions:

- Analyze CRM history and segment
- Generate personalized messages
- Initiate multi-channel (SMS/email) campaigns

React based on user response (text classification, sentiment)

iv). Scheduling Agent
Purpose: Manage calendar, availability, and booking
Functions:

- Suggest slots based on rules

- Send reminders
- Update calendars upon confirmed bookings

v) Feedback & Sentiment Agent

Purpose: Gather and classify customer feedback post-purchase or post-service
Functions:

- Send NPS-style questions
- Classify responses as promoters/passives/detractors

6. Review Request Agent

Purpose: Ask for public reviews (Google, Yelp, etc.)
Functions:

- Trigger only for promoters
- Personalize messages
- Remind if not submitted

7. Review Response Agent

Purpose: Monitor and respond to reviews publicly
Functions:

- Draft polite and brand-aligned responses
- Escalate negative reviews to support team
- Track reputation score

8. Referral Generator Agent

Purpose: Activate happy customers to refer friends
Functions:

- Offer rewards or incentives
- Handle referral link delivery

- Monitor lead conversion from referrals

9. Orchestrator Agent
Purpose: Coordinate the above agents for seamless workflow
Functions:

- Enforce rules (e.g., if no reply in 2 days, re-send)
- Prioritize actions based on engagement score
- Monitor agent health and performance

10. Analytics & Learning Agent
Purpose: Continuously learn from campaign data
Functions:

- Measure open rates, CTRs, conversions
- Suggest campaign changes
- Train other agents via feedback loop

Key Technologies for Implementation

- LLMs: For conversation, content creation, review responses
- RAG (Retrieval Augmented Generation): For CRM-specific messaging
- LangChain / AutoGen / CrewAI: To structure multi-agent orchestration
- GoHighLevel API Integration: For backend automation
- Twilio / SendGrid: For SMS and Email campaign execution

Benefits of the Agentic Model

- Autonomy: Each agent operates independently on assigned goals.
- Scalability: Add more agents (like Ad Buyer Agent or Social Media Agent) without disrupting the ecosystem.
- Adaptability: Agents improve via feedback, sentiment, and performance data.
- Reduced Human Oversight: Minimal manual intervention required.

Takeaway

AI is a game-changer for startups looking to scale their marketing and sales efforts. By automating repetitive tasks, gaining deeper insights into customer behavior, and personalizing campaigns at scale, startups can maximize their impact and efficiency. As AI technologies continue to evolve, startups must embrace these advancements to stay competitive in an ever-changing market.

CHAPTER TEN

Scaling Operations with AI and Automation

Introduction

As a startup grows, operational efficiency becomes increasingly critical. The challenge lies in maintaining productivity and customer satisfaction while scaling up resources, managing increased workloads, and minimizing operational costs. This is where AI and automation play a pivotal role. AI-driven tools can help startups streamline operations, reduce manual tasks, improve accuracy, and make data-driven decisions that can help scale operations seamlessly.

This chapter explores how startups can leverage AI and automation to scale their operations effectively, ensuring they have the right infrastructure, tools, and processes to handle growth without compromising quality.

10.1 The Role of AI in Operational Efficiency

AI can drive operational efficiency across several domains, from workflow automation to predictive analytics, and real-time decision-making. By using AI, startups can handle increased complexity, minimize human errors, and optimize resource allocation.

1. Workflow Automation

- Task Automation: Routine tasks such as data entry, invoice generation, scheduling, and customer service responses can be automated using AI. Tools like Zapier or Integromat enable startups to create automated workflows across apps and services, ensuring tasks are completed without human intervention.
- Robotic Process Automation (RPA): RPA tools like UiPath and Automation Anywhere use AI to automate repetitive processes like payroll, HR management, and supply chain coordination. This reduces the need for manual intervention, freeing up time for more strategic initiatives.
- Document Processing: AI-powered document management systems like DocuSign and Adobe Sign automate document handling, approval workflows, and contract management. AI can read, understand, and categorize documents to ensure faster and more efficient workflows.

2. Real-Time Data Processing

- Data Analysis for Decision Making: AI can analyze vast amounts of operational data in real-time and provide actionable insights to help startups make informed decisions. This could include inventory management, employee performance, customer feedback, and sales data.

- Supply Chain Management: AI tools like Llamasoft and Blue Yonder enable startups to optimize their supply chain by forecasting demand, predicting potential disruptions, and suggesting the best routes or suppliers. This can reduce costs, improve delivery times, and ensure better inventory management.
- Demand Forecasting: By analyzing past sales and market trends, AI can predict future demand for products and services, ensuring that inventory and resources are optimized accordingly.

10.2 AI-Powered Customer Service and Support

Providing exceptional customer service is crucial as startups scale. AI-driven customer support systems can enhance the customer experience while reducing costs and response times.

1. AI Chatbots for Customer Support

- Automating Customer Queries: Chatbots like Zendesk, Drift, and Intercom are powered by AI to provide instant responses to customer queries, 24/7. These chatbots use NLP (Natural Language Processing) to understand and resolve issues efficiently.
- Personalized Customer Experience: AI chatbots can also learn from past customer interactions, ensuring that responses are increasingly personalized over time, leading to better customer satisfaction and faster resolution times.
- Multichannel Support: AI systems can handle support requests across multiple channels, including email, social media, and messaging apps, ensuring consistent and unified customer service.

2. AI for Knowledge Management

- AI-Powered Help Desks: Solutions like Freshdesk or Zoho Desk use AI to categorize and resolve support tickets, providing customers with immediate assistance. The system can learn from each interaction and recommend solutions based on customer history.
- Automated Knowledge Base: AI can create and maintain a dynamic knowledge base that updates itself as new issues arise and solutions are found. This allows both customers and support staff to access relevant information quickly, ensuring faster problem resolution.

10.3 Streamlining Financial Operations with AI

Financial management is one of the most critical areas for startups to scale effectively. AI-driven tools can automate routine financial tasks and provide valuable insights for better financial decision-making.

1. AI for Accounting and Bookkeeping

- Automating Bookkeeping: AI-powered tools like QuickBooks and Xero automate accounting tasks such as transaction categorization, invoice creation, and tax calculations, ensuring accurate financial records with minimal manual effort.
- Expense Management: AI-driven tools like Expensify use machine learning to analyze receipts, categorize expenses, and even flag unusual transactions, improving financial visibility and reducing administrative overhead.

2. Financial Forecasting

- Cash Flow Management: AI-based tools can help forecast cash flow, ensuring that startups have adequate funds to handle expenses, investments, and growth. Platforms like Float and Fathom provide cash flow predictions and financial health assessments based on historical data.
- Investment Analysis: AI tools like Kavout and Alpaca help startups make data-driven investment decisions, by analyzing stock market data, identifying trends, and providing predictive analytics on market movements.

10.4 AI for Human Resource Management

As startups grow, managing employees and talent becomes more complex. AI and automation tools can assist in streamlining HR processes, improving recruitment, and enhancing employee engagement.

1. Automated Recruitment

- AI-Powered Hiring: AI-driven tools like HireVue and Jobvite automate the recruitment process by screening resumes, analyzing candidates' skills, and even conducting initial interview rounds through AI chatbots.
- Predictive Hiring: By analyzing historical hiring data, AI can predict which candidates are most likely to succeed in specific roles. This helps startups make data-driven decisions, reducing bias and increasing the quality of hires.
- Employee Onboarding: AI-powered onboarding systems like BambooHR can automate the administrative aspects of onboarding, such as document submission, policy review, and benefits enrollment.

2. Employee Engagement and Retention

- AI for Employee Sentiment Analysis: AI tools like CultureAmp and Workday use sentiment analysis to track employee satisfaction through surveys, feedback, and engagement metrics. This data can help startups identify areas of improvement and take action to reduce turnover rates.
- Personalized Learning and Development: AI-powered learning platforms such as EdCast and Coursera tailor training content to individual employees' learning styles and career goals, increasing employee engagement and boosting performance.

10.5 Optimizing Supply Chain and Inventory Management with AI

Efficient supply chain and inventory management are essential for scaling operations smoothly. AI can optimize logistics, predict demand, and automate procurement processes.

1. AI for Inventory Management

- Predictive Inventory Restocking: AI tools like TradeGecko and NetSuite predict when inventory will run low and automate reordering, reducing the chances of stockouts or overstocking.
- Warehouse Automation: AI-powered robots and drones can streamline warehouse operations, moving products to the right location based on demand forecasts. Locus and Fetch Robotics are examples of AI-driven platforms that optimize warehouse management.

2. AI for Logistics Optimization

- Route Optimization: AI can optimize delivery routes, ensuring faster and more cost-effective transportation. Platforms like Route4Me and OptimoRoute use machine learning to analyze traffic patterns,
- delivery windows, and vehicle capacities to minimize delivery costs and improve service reliability.
- Demand Forecasting for Supply Chain: AI platforms help predict supply and demand fluctuations by analyzing trends, historical data, and external factors such as weather or geopolitical events. This allows startups to adjust their supply chain strategy to maintain optimal inventory levels.

10.6 Best Practices for Implementing AI in Operations
While AI offers numerous benefits, successful implementation requires careful planning and execution. Here are some best practices for startups looking to leverage AI in their operations:

- Identify the Right Areas for AI: Focus on high-impact areas that can benefit from automation, such as customer service, supply chain, HR, and financial operations. Start with one or two processes and scale as the company grows.
- Invest in Quality Data: AI is only effective when it has access to high-quality data. Ensure your data is clean, consistent, and organized before implementing AI tools.
- Employee Training and Buy-in: Educate employees about AI and automation tools, ensuring they understand how these technologies will help them do their jobs more efficiently rather than replacing them.
- Monitor AI Performance: Continuously assess the performance of AI tools to ensure they are delivering

the desired outcomes. Regularly refine and optimize the systems as needed.

- Security and Compliance: Ensure that AI tools comply with industry regulations, such as GDPR or HIPAA, and that all data is secured and protected.

10.7 The Future of AI in Scaling Operations

The role of AI in scaling operations will continue to evolve as AI technologies become more advanced. From predictive analytics to autonomous decision-making, AI will play an increasingly crucial role in streamlining operations, reducing costs, and driving business growth. As AI becomes more integrated into business processes, startups will be able to scale faster, more efficiently, and with greater agility than ever before.

Takeaway

AI is not just a tool for startups to increase their productivity—it is a catalyst for scaling operations in a way that was once thought impossible. By embracing automation, predictive analytics, and intelligent systems, startups can streamline processes, reduce costs, and focus on growth. As AI continues to evolve, the future of startup operations will be defined by faster, smarter, and more efficient workflows.

CHAPTER ELEVEN

Building a Data-Driven Culture for Long-Term Success

Introduction

In today's hyper-competitive environment, intuition alone isn't enough to drive business success. Startups that embed data into their decision-making processes are more agile, precise, and customer-focused. A data-driven culture enables organizations to harness insights, validate hypotheses, test assumptions, and continuously learn and evolve. For a resource-constrained startup, this culture is not just a luxury — it's a growth multiplier.

This chapter outlines how startups can build and sustain a data-driven culture that aligns with their strategic objectives, fuels innovation, and supports intelligent scaling.

11.1 What is a Data-Driven Culture?

A data-driven culture is one where decisions at every level — from product development to marketing, hiring, and customer experience — are made based on data analysis and insights, rather than guesswork or hierarchy.

Key characteristics:

- Everyone relies on data, not just data teams.
- Data is accessible and democratized across departments.
- There's clarity on what to measure (KPIs, OKRs).
- Curiosity and experimentation are encouraged.
- Decisions are tested and validated by evidence.
- Leaders lead by example and demand data-backed justifications.
- A true data culture means even the smallest decisions — like the timing of a push notification or the copy of a landing page — are grounded in measurable insights.

11.2 Why Startups Need a Data-Driven Culture Early

Startups face high uncertainty and rapid change. A data-driven approach helps mitigate these risks by bringing clarity and speed to decision-making.

Benefits include:

- Agility: Fast feedback loops reduce risk and allow for quick pivots.
- Efficiency: Scarce resources are directed where ROI is proven.
- Investor Confidence: VCs favor startups with measurable, defensible traction.
- Customer Centricity: Data reveals what customers want, how they behave, and where friction lies.

- Faster Iteration: Continuous testing and learning lead to product-market fit.
- Early investment in data capabilities often distinguishes unicorns from startups that plateau.

11.3 Building Blocks of a Data-Driven Startup
1. Clear Metrics and KPIs

- Define your North Star Metric (e.g., Daily Active Users, MRR).
- Align departmental KPIs to overarching business goals.
- Distinguish between leading (predictive) and lagging (historical) indicators.

Example (for a SaaS company):

- North Star: Monthly Active Users (MAUs)
- Marketing KPI: Customer Acquisition Cost (CAC)
- Product KPI: Feature Adoption Rate
- Support KPI: Average Resolution Time

2. Robust Data Infrastructure
Even with limited budgets, choose scalable, modular tools:

- Data Warehouse: BigQuery, Snowflake, AWS Redshift
- Analytics & Tracking: Mixpanel, Google Analytics, Amplitude, Segment
- Visualization: Metabase, Looker, Tableau, Power BI
- ETL & Pipelines: Fivetran, Airbyte, dbt (data build tool)

3. Data Literacy Across Teams

- Offer training on data interpretation and dashboards.
- Promote a shared vocabulary (via a data glossary).
- Encourage hypotheses, exploration, and asking "why" in every decision.
- Celebrate data-led decisions publicly.

11.4 Cultivating a Culture of Experimentation

Startups thrive when they test and learn continuously. With data:

- A/B Testing: Compare variants in marketing, UI, pricing, etc.
- Cohort Analysis: See how different user groups behave over time.
- Post-Mortems: After every campaign, analyze what worked, what didn't, and why.
- Controlled Experiments: Run tests with control groups for more accurate learnings.
- "Failure is data in disguise. Learn from it."
- Encourage teams to treat every decision as a hypothesis to test — not a certainty.

11.5 Democratizing Access to Data

- Democratization empowers faster, informed decisions at all levels.
- Build role-specific dashboards with KPIs tailored to each function.
- Share auto-generated reports via Slack, Teams, or email.
- Promote self-service analytics so teams can explore without bottlenecks.
- Use data catalogs to help users find and understand datasets.

- Encouraging data access builds trust and transparency while reducing reliance on specialized analysts.

11.6 Using Data to Personalize Customer Experience

Customers expect personalization — and data makes it possible:

- Behavioral Data: Track in-app activity and usage patterns.
- Demographic Data: Understand user segments and preferences.
- Transactional Data: Analyze past purchases, frequency, and value.

AI-powered personalization can:

- Recommend content or products.
- Trigger onboarding flows or reminders.
- Deliver personalized marketing and support interactions.
- Real-time data enables you to meet customers where they are, with what they need — exactly when they need it.

11.7 Building Feedback Loops

Continuous learning requires continuous feedback:

- Customer Feedback: NPS, CSAT, app reviews, support tickets, user interviews.
- Team Feedback: Internal retrospectives, 360 feedback, and pulse surveys.
- Product Feedback: Usage data, heatmaps, feature requests, drop-off rates.

- Use this input to refine features, messaging, onboarding, and more. Close the loop by acting on the feedback and showing users that their voice matters.

11.8 Privacy, Ethics, and Governance

A data-driven culture must be a responsible one:

- Build with privacy-first principles (GDPR, CCPA compliance).
- Clearly explain how data is used — earn user trust.
- Audit AI models for bias, drift, and unintended consequences.
- Implement data retention policies, access controls, and audit trails.
- "Just because you can collect the data doesn't mean you should."
- Good governance earns user trust and protects your brand.

11.9 Case Studies

1. Airbnb

Used data science to fine-tune pricing, A/B test UI changes, and improve search algorithms. Their "Data University" initiative trained non-technical teams to use data tools effectively.

2. Razorpay

Runs real-time fraud detection systems and dashboards to monitor operations across payment, lending, and banking platforms.

3. Notion

Tracks feature engagement and user journeys to prioritize product development, balancing qualitative feedback with quantitative usage data.

4. Swiggy

Optimizes delivery routes, pricing, and recommendations using real-time data across millions of orders.

5. Duolingo

A/B tests every single lesson and UX flow — leading to higher retention and more effective learning.

11.10 Action Plan to Build a Data-Driven Startup

- Set Clear Goals: Define OKRs and KPIs from Day 1.
- Invest in Tools: Use affordable tools like Mixpanel, Metabase, and Airbyte.
- Upskill the Team: Incorporate data training in onboarding and L&D programs.
- Reward Data Use: Acknowledge and promote data-led wins.
- Review Regularly: Use monthly dashboards and review meetings to improve continuously.
- Appoint a Data Champion: Someone to lead initiatives and ensure adoption.

Conclusion

A data-driven culture is not about dashboards and KPIs alone — it's about transforming how people think, decide, and act. It empowers your team to move with confidence, adapt rapidly, and build what truly matters. In an uncertain world, data is your compass — helping you navigate toward growth, product-market fit, and meaningful impact.

Building a data-driven culture is one of the most powerful steps a startup can take. It improves clarity, reduces waste, enhances decision-making, and unlocks sustained growth. With the right mindset, tools, and leadership commitment, any startup — no matter how small — can build its future on the firm foundation of data. Start small. Start now. The returns will compound.

CHAPTER TWELVE

CREATING TECH-ENABLED BUSINESS MODELS AND MONETIZATION STRATEGIES

Introduction

Technology is no longer just a function—it is the business model. In today's digital era, the smartest startups don't just use tech to build apps—they use it to disrupt markets, scale rapidly, cut costs, personalize experiences, and monetize effectively. The right tech-enabled business model can differentiate your startup, unlock new revenue streams, and dramatically improve your ROI.

This chapter guides you through how to design lean, technology-powered business models and monetization strategies that are scalable, defensible, and profitable.

12.1 Understanding Tech-Enabled Business Models

A tech-enabled business model leverages digital technologies to deliver core value propositions more efficiently, at scale, or in a more personalized way than traditional alternatives.

<u>**Common Tech-Enabled Models for Startups:**</u>

Common Tech-Enabled Models for Startups:

Model	Description	Examples
Platform Model	Connects two or more user groups (e.g., buyers and sellers)	Uber, Airbnb, UrbanClap
Freemium to Paid	Offer free basic tier, charge for premium	Notion, Canva, Dropbox
Subscription SaaS	Monthly or annual payments for cloud-based software	Zoho, RazorpayX
On-Demand Services	Real-time service delivery via app/platform	Swiggy, Zepto
Marketplace Aggregator	Centralized digital marketplace	Flipkart, Amazon
API-as-a-Product	Monetizing backend capabilities via APIs	Twilio, Razorpay, Stripe
Licensing Model	Charge for software/IP use (good for enterprise deals)	Microsoft Dynamics, ERPNext
Data Monetization	Anonymized analytics or insights sold or shared	Credit bureaus, AdTech tools

Common Technology based Models

12.2 Designing Lean Business Models for Maximum ROI

Tech allows startups to eliminate intermediaries, automate processes, and scale fast with fewer people.

Tips for High-ROI Business Design:

? <u>Use No-Code/Low-Code Tools</u>

- Tools like Bubble, Glide, Zapier, and Webflow let you build apps, workflows, and sites without heavy dev cost.

- MVPs can be launched 10x faster and cheaper.

? <u>Go Direct-to-Consumer (D2C)</u>

- Cut out distributors and retailers using e-commerce platforms like Shopify, Instamojo, Dukaan.
- Use WhatsApp Business API or Instagram Shops for mobile-first commerce.

? <u>Cloud-Based Infrastructure</u>

- Replace upfront capex (servers, licenses) with pay-as-you-go cloud tools: AWS, Firebase, Vercel, or DigitalOcean.
- Use scalable serverless functions (e.g., AWS Lambda).

? <u>Microservices and APIs</u>

- Build only what's unique—integrate the rest.
- Use payment APIs (Razorpay), auth (Auth0), comms (Twilio), storage (Cloudinary), etc.

? <u>Automate First, Hire Later</u>

- Use chatbots, CRM automation, RPA tools, and AI assistants instead of early hires.
- Marketing automation tools: Mailchimp, MoEngage, Customer.io.

12.3 Monetization Strategy for Startups: Lean and Smart

Your product may solve a real problem—but unless you monetize it right, you're not building a business. Smart monetization blends user psychology, customer segment needs, and technology.

12.3.1 Key Questions to Answer First

- Who pays, and why?
- When do they pay? (Before, during, after usage?)
- What are they comparing you to? (Price anchoring)
- What do they see as "value delivered"?

12.4 Proven Monetization Models for Startups
1. Freemium + Paywall

- Free basic version to acquire users, charge for extra features, storage, or users.
- Tools: Notion, Zoom, Grammarly.
- Low Cost + High ROI Strategy:
- Use free users for word-of-mouth and SEO.
- Convert 2–5% to paid plans.

Tips:

- Time-limited premium trials work better than forever-free.
- Trigger upgrades via in-app nudges.

2. Tiered Subscription Plans

- Simple monthly pricing tiers based on usage or value.
- Good for SaaS, analytics tools, marketplaces.

Startup ROI Boost:

- Use pricing psychology: decoy pricing, charm pricing, and anchoring.
- Offer annual plans at discount for upfront cash flow.

3. Usage-Based Pricing

- Pay-per-use model for APIs, tools, or logistics.
- Fair, scalable, and attractive to SMBs.

Examples: Razorpay, Postman, Amazon AWS.
4. Marketplace Commission Model

- Charge commission on every transaction.
- You host the ecosystem; value lies in aggregation, trust, and UX.

Low Cost Tip: Use ready-made marketplace frameworks (Sharetribe, Arcadier) for MVPs.
5. Licensing and White-Labeling

- Offer core tech/IP to others under a licensing deal.
- Great for deep tech, fintech, healthtech, and B2B

Advantages:

- No need to acquire end-users yourself.
- High-margin B2B revenues.

6. Affiliate or Referral Revenue

- Get a cut from third-party sales via your platform.
- Good for content platforms, community-led startups, fintechs.

Examples: Cred (offers), CashKaro, Finshots.

7. Embedded Finance / Fintech Layer

If you have a B2B/B2C platform, add credit, insurance, or wallets.

Examples:

- RazorpayX added payroll and vendor payments.
- Ola added insurance and credit card options.
- Tools: Setu, Open, Decentro (India).

12.5 Smart Pricing Hacks for Startups

- Anchor High, Offer Smart Discounts
- Show ₹4,999 crossed out, offer ₹1,499.
- Bundle Services to increase perceived value.
- Offer Outcome-Based Pricing where possible (e.g., per lead, per result).
- Let Customers Choose: Add "Pay what you want" or donation-based pricing for trials or MVPs.
- Dynamic Pricing: Use AI tools or customer segmentation for personalized pricing (e.g., Chargebee, Stripe).

12.6 Tech Stack Recommendations for Monetization

Given below is the tech Stack Recommendations for Monetization, organized by functionality and tailored for startups aiming for high ROI and low cost:

1. Payments

- To accept payments from customers securely and efficiently, especially for online transactions, you'll need a payment gateway.

- Razorpay – One of the most popular options in India, offering fast integration for websites and mobile apps. It supports UPI, cards, net banking, and subscription billing.
- Stripe – Ideal for global startups. Known for its developer-friendly APIs and support for SaaS-style recurring billing.
- Instamojo – A great low-code option for small businesses and creators. Simple to set up and supports payment links and digital store features.

2. Subscriptions

- If your monetization model includes recurring payments, a subscription management tool is critical.
- Chargebee – A powerful tool that handles recurring billing, invoicing, trials, coupons, and more. It integrates easily with payment gateways and accounting software.
- Paddle – Especially good for global SaaS startups. It handles compliance, taxes, and cross-border subscriptions.
- Zoho Subscriptions – Part of the Zoho suite, ideal for Indian SaaS businesses looking for affordable, integrated billing systems.

3. CRM + Email Marketing

- To manage customer relationships, segment users, and run targeted email campaigns to increase conversions.
- HubSpot Free – Offers CRM, email marketing, forms, and basic automation in the free version—perfect for early-stage startups.

- Brevo (formerly Sendinblue) – A cost-effective email and SMS marketing platform with automation features.
- Mailchimp – Popular with startups for its ease of use, templates, and marketing automation (free for up to 500 contacts).

4. Chatbots

- To automate customer support, lead capture, and onboarding without needing a support team available 24/7.
- Tidio – Combines live chat and AI-powered chatbot features. Easy to integrate with websites.
- Crisp – A multichannel customer messaging tool that includes bots, knowledge base, and shared inboxes.
- Botpress – An open-source, customizable chatbot framework for developers who want more control over logic.

5. No-Code App Builders

- To rapidly prototype or build MVPs without writing code.
- Glide – Turns Google Sheets into powerful mobile and web apps with a drag-and-drop interface.
- Bubble – One of the most powerful no-code platforms, allowing you to build fully functional web apps.
- Adalo – Focused on mobile-first apps with drag-and-drop UI and backend database features.

6. Analytics

- To track user behavior, acquisition channels, and conversion funnels to optimize ROI.
- Google Analytics – The most widely used free tool for tracking website/app traffic and user behavior.
- Hotjar – Provides heatmaps, session recordings, and feedback tools to understand user interaction.
- Mixpanel – Offers advanced product analytics, funnel tracking, and cohort analysis for SaaS and app startups.

7. Heatmaps

- To visualize where users are clicking or dropping off on your site.
- Clarity (by Microsoft) – A free and powerful heatmap and session recording tool with no traffic limits.
- Smartlook – Combines heatmaps, user session replays, and event tracking for deeper user experience analysis.

8. Referral Programs

- To incentivize existing users to refer new customers and grow virally.
- Viral Loops – A plug-and-play referral marketing tool modeled after successful campaigns like Dropbox's.
- InviteReferrals – Easy to implement with customizable widgets, especially for eCommerce and apps.

9. Affiliate Marketing

- To allow other partners or websites to promote your product for a commission.
- Tapfiliate – A popular affiliate tracking software for SaaS and eCommerce businesses.

- FirstPromoter – Designed for SaaS businesses with integrations into Stripe and Paddle to track affiliate conversions and payouts automatically.

Each of these tools is selected for its ability to help startups scale revenue, automate processes, and reduce time-to-market, all while staying cost-efficient.

12.7 Case Studies: Lean Tech, Smart Monetization

Case 1: Sleep Klinics (Healthtech)

- Tech-enabled diagnosis with minimal in-person interaction.
- Monetized CPAP machines + home care services.
- Used WhatsApp + Teleconsultation + 10% commission model.

Case 2: Kuku FM (India)

- Freemium audio content platform.
- Monetized with subscription at ₹99/month after free trials.
- Heavy use of WhatsApp drip marketing + referrals.

Case 3: Razorpay

- Monetized APIs, then built platform revenue via RazorpayX.
- Added lending, payroll, insurance—embedding finance.

12.8 Action Plan for Startups: Building Monetization into Your Tech

Step wise Action plan:

- Validate willingness to pay before scaling features
- Choose tech stack that supports pricing and payments
- Test 2–3 pricing models (freemium, per-use, tiered)
- Run A/B tests on plan names, prices, and benefits
- Build dashboards to track CAC, LTV, churn, ROI
- Automate billing, dunning emails, and retention flows

Conclusion

Tech-enabled business models are not just about innovation—they are about scalability, unit economics, and customer-centric monetization. Startups that build lean but powerful digital business models gain the agility to pivot, scale, and monetize fast—all while keeping operational costs low.

By combining the right technologies with a deep understanding of your customer journey and strategic pricing, your startup can become both efficient and unstoppable.

CHAPTER THIRTEEN

Unlocking Startup Potential with the Metaverse and Digital Twins

Startups today are navigating an era where immersive digital experiences and real-time data intelligence are no longer futuristic ideals—they are active business tools. Two such transformative technologies are the Metaverse and Digital Twins. These aren't just tech trends—they're practical innovations with massive implications for how startups can engage customers, deliver services, train teams, and scale operations. Whether you're building a healthcare platform, an edtech solution, a retail business, or even a factory automation service, these tools offer accessible and scalable ways to revolutionize user experience, improve efficiency, and monetize digital value—often on a shoestring budget.

Understanding the Metaverse

The Metaverse refers to a persistent 3D virtual world that merges digital and physical experiences. It creates immersive environments through technologies like Augmented Reality (AR), Virtual Reality (VR), digital avatars, blockchain/tokenization, and AI-driven interactions. What makes the Metaverse powerful for startups is that it's accessible across devices—mobile phones, desktops, and immersive gear like the Oculus Rift or Apple Vision Pro. In this world, users can interact, work, shop, learn, play, and socialize—mirroring and often enhancing real-world activities. This opens doors for startups to design virtual clinics, online shopping malls, virtual schools, or product testing environments that transcend geography.

Understanding Digital Twins

A Digital Twin is a real-time, virtual model of a physical entity—be it a product, person, process, or system—connected via IoT (Internet of Things) and powered by real-time data and AI analytics. Digital twins enable continuous monitoring, optimization, and prediction. In healthcare, they can replicate a patient's physiological data for remote monitoring or simulations. In retail, they can track and analyze customer behavior within a virtual store. In manufacturing, they can forecast machinery failures or optimize production layouts. These virtual replicas enable startups to prototype smarter, react faster, and innovate cheaper.

Why These Technologies Matter for Startups

Startups, often agile but budget-conscious, can significantly benefit from these tools in several impactful ways:

- Enhanced Customer Experience: Immersive onboarding or virtual showrooms help increase engagement and retention.
- Training & Education: Using VR/AR for employee or customer training reduces costs and boosts knowledge retention.
- Remote Collaboration: Virtual HQs, events, and meetings enhance engagement in distributed teams.
- Product Demonstrations: Real-time simulation of product usage helps secure faster and more confident buy-ins.
- Real-Time Monitoring: Whether it's logistics, health, or sales, digital twins allow startups to optimize and troubleshoot proactively.

Domain-Specific Use Cases
<u>Healthcare</u>

- Virtual clinics and ICUs, where doctors and patients meet in the Metaverse.
- Digital twins of patients for tracking vitals remotely.
- Mental health therapy through virtual avatars in immersive settings.

<u>Education & Training</u>

- VR classrooms where learning is immersive and gamified.

- Avatars and AI tutors create highly personalized, interactive experiences.

Retail & eCommerce

- Virtual stores and dressing rooms that allow users to "try before buying."
- Behavioral simulation using customer avatars to optimize store layouts and sales journeys.

Real Estate

- Virtual 3D property tours for potential buyers from anywhere in the world.
- Smart building systems with digital twins for predictive maintenance and energy savings.

Industry & Manufacturing

- Factory twins to forecast maintenance needs, boost safety, and streamline operations.
- Remote control of equipment using AR/VR tools for real-time response and quality control.

Free & Open-Source Tools for the Metaverse and Digital Twins

You don't need massive budgets to explore these tech innovations. Several free and open-source tools can help startups get started:

- Mozilla Hubs: Build free virtual worlds directly in the browser—great for meetings or demo spaces.

- JanusXR: Web-based VR platform to create open Metaverse environments.
- FrameVR: Easily customizable 3D collaborative spaces.
- A-Frame: A web framework to create VR scenes and environments with simple HTML.
- FIWARE: A powerful open-source framework for smart cities and digital twin development.
- Blender + Unreal Engine: Design and simulate 3D products or environments in photorealistic detail.

Low-Cost Ways Startups Can Begin
You can dip your toes into the Metaverse and Digital Twin world without major investment:

- Virtual Offices: Use Mozilla Hubs or Gather to host your startup's virtual workplace.
- Digital Product Demos: Build interactive VR experiences using Unity or A-Frame.
- Simulate Operations: Connect IoT devices to FIWARE for logistics or operations monitoring.
- Training & Onboarding: Deploy virtual simulations and Metaverse avatars for team training.
- Customer Engagement: Host virtual events, consultations, or product launches in immersive 3D spaces.

Monetization Models for Startups
The Metaverse and Digital Twins also open up new revenue models:

- Virtual Products & NFTs: Sell branded merchandise, digital services, or experiences in 3D.

- Virtual Real Estate: Rent or sell your brand's presence in the Metaverse for events or customer experiences.
- Subscription Access: Offer exclusive access to virtual clinics, learning platforms, or simulation tools.
- Advertising & Sponsorships: Monetize virtual spaces through branded experiences and placements.
- Digital Twin Licensing: Build and license replicas of industry-specific systems or processes to others.
- Best Practices for Startup Implementation
- To make the most of these tools, startups should:
- Start Small: Choose a narrow, focused use case that addresses a clear need.
- Ensure Mobile Compatibility: Many users access Metaverse environments through smartphones.
- Prioritize Data Integration: Ensure virtual environments connect with your core data systems for real value.
- Focus on User Onboarding: Make entry simple and guided with tutorials and helpful avatars.
- Iterate Based on Feedback: Launch early, gather user input, refine, and expand.

<u>Startup Case Study: TeleCareVerse</u>

One example of a successful startup application is TeleCareVerse, a virtual clinic built using Mozilla Hubs. The platform allows doctors to appear as avatars and interact with patients in immersive settings. Patients also have avatars, with real-time health vitals linked through wearables and digital twins. The startup monetized its services via virtual consultations, subscription-based health services, and affiliate diagnostic partnerships. It's a clear example of how innovative technologies can transform traditional healthcare delivery, even on a lean budget.

Conclusion

For startups aiming to break through today's crowded and competitive landscape, the Metaverse and Digital Twins offer a game-changing opportunity. They make it possible to design better user experiences, launch smarter operations, train faster, and sell more—all in a virtual or hybrid environment that scales cost-effectively. With free tools, open-source frameworks, and creative use cases, the barrier to entry is lower than ever. Startups that embrace this shift early can go from being digital participants to digital pioneers.

BUILDING AND LEADING A HIGH-IMPACT TECH-DRIVEN TEAM

In today's fast-paced digital economy, building a high-performing, tech-driven team is not just about hiring the best developers or data scientists — it's about creating a culture of innovation, agility, and purpose. For startups, where every hire can significantly influence growth, the quality and synergy of the team determine whether the product succeeds, pivots, or fails. This chapter explores how to build and lead such a team effectively.

14.1 The Foundation: Vision, Mission & Tech Culture

Every strong team starts with a clear vision and mission. When your startup has a well-articulated purpose — like "democratizing healthcare access using AI" or "creating immersive education experiences through AR/VR" — it naturally attracts aligned talent. A tech-driven culture emphasizes not just coding but curiosity, data-driven decisions, and continuous learning.

For example, at a healthtech startup, the mission might be to reduce ICU mortality by 30% using AI-enabled monitoring. This clarity helps attract team members who are passionate about healthcare and technology.

A strong tech culture also involves transparency, experimentation, and openness to failure. Organizations like Netflix and GitLab are known for their clear communication, freedom with responsibility, and "blameless post-mortems" when things go wrong.

14.2 Roles and Structure in a Tech-Driven Startup

While titles can vary, most tech startups need a core set of roles to drive innovation and execution:

- Tech/Product Founder or CTO – Sets the technology direction, architecture, and innovation roadmap.
- Developers (Frontend, Backend, Full Stack) – Build the core product or platform.
- UX/UI Designers – Ensure the product is usable and delightful.
- Data Analysts/Data Scientists – Make data actionable, build AI/ML models if needed.
- DevOps Engineers – Automate deployments, manage cloud infrastructure.
- Product Managers – Bridge customer needs with technical execution.

In early stages, people often wear multiple hats. For instance, a full-stack developer might also handle DevOps or early QA. As the company grows, specialization becomes important.

A practical example is a SaaS fintech platform, where a lean team may initially consist of:

- One tech lead who handles architecture and backend
- One frontend developer
- One UI/UX designer
- One business co-founder who also doubles up as the product manager
- As the platform scales, roles get split further to ensure speed and quality.

14.3 Hiring for Attitude, Learning, and Values

In startups, technical skills are essential, but attitude, adaptability, and cultural fit are even more crucial. The best team members are those who are:

- Hungry to learn
- Excited by the mission
- Willing to step outside their comfort zone
- A great question during hiring might be: "Tell me about a time you had to learn a new technology in a short time — how did you approach it?" This surfaces problem-solving attitude and passion.

In a small team, one toxic or unmotivated hire can derail productivity. Conversely, hiring even a junior engineer who is curious, collaborative, and mission-driven can add exponential value over time.

14.4 Leadership in a Tech Startup: Not Just Management

Leadership in a tech startup isn't about hierarchy or control — it's about empowerment, clarity, and empathy. A good tech leader:

- Communicates clearly
- Removes blockers
- Balances innovation with execution
- Coaches the team, not commands

For example, a tech lead at an edtech startup may not write all the code but will guide junior developers, align with the product team, and ensure technical debt doesn't accumulate.

Empathy is crucial. In fast-moving teams, burnout and stress are real. Regular 1-on-1s, team retrospectives, and mental health check-ins go a long way in building trust.

14.5 Agile and Lean Execution Models

Startups must execute fast — and learn faster. Agile methodologies like Scrum or Kanban enable iterative development, short feedback loops, and real-time adaptability. Weekly sprints, daily stand-ups, and biweekly demos help ensure alignment.

For example, a startup building an AI chatbot might:

- Run 2-week sprints
- Deploy updates every Friday
- Use Jira/Trello for task tracking
- Run user testing with real users every 2 sprints

Lean development also means focusing on Minimum Viable Products (MVPs). Instead of spending 6 months building a complex platform, release a basic version in 4 weeks, test it, and improve based on feedback.

14.6 Tools to Boost Tech Team Productivity

A tech-driven team thrives on the right stack. Some commonly used tools include:

- Version Control: Git + GitHub/GitLab
- CI/CD: Jenkins, GitHub Actions
- Project Management: Trello, Jira, Notion
- Communication: Slack, Discord, Zoom
- Design & Prototyping: Figma, Adobe XD
- Code Collaboration: Visual Studio Code with Live Share
- Using automation (for tests, deployment, bug tracking) allows small teams to punch above their weight.

14.7 Remote & Hybrid Teams: Making It Work

With global talent and distributed teams becoming the norm, asynchronous collaboration and documentation become critical.

Best practices include:

- Clear OKRs and weekly goals
- Daily stand-up messages on Slack
- Detailed documentation in Notion or Confluence
- Regular virtual team-building activities

For example, a startup with developers in India, a designer in Ukraine, and a product manager in Canada can still thrive — provided alignment, time zone sensitivity, and communication norms are established.

14.8 Retaining & Growing Talent

Once you build a great team, retaining them becomes a priority. Growth, recognition, and ownership are powerful motivators.

Ways to retain talent:

- Stock options or equity for long-term wealth sharing
- Learning budgets for upskilling (e.g., Coursera, Udemy, conferences)

- Career roadmaps for engineers and designers
- Transparent communication about business direction and wins

An example: At a health AI startup, developers were allowed to co-author research papers and present at AI conferences — this boosted motivation and retention.

14.9 Case Study: Building a Fintech Engineering Team

A fintech startup aimed to build a mobile-first lending platform for rural India. The founding team began with:

- 1 product-focused CTO
- 1 React Native developer
- 1 backend (Node.js) developer
- 1 DevOps freelancer

They used open-source technologies, daily stand-ups on WhatsApp, and Firebase for real-time database management. As they scaled to 100,000 users, they onboarded:

- A QA lead
- A machine learning engineer
- A customer support lead trained in basic tech
- The CEO regularly held "Tech Townhalls" to keep the whole company in sync, which built strong alignment and loyalty.

Conclusion

Building and leading a high-impact tech-driven team is both an art and a science. It requires clarity of purpose, empathy in leadership, a bias for execution, and a deep respect for talent. For startups especially, the right team can mean the difference between a pivot and a breakthrough. Focus on hiring for attitude, enabling through systems, and leading with heart — and your tech team will drive innovation that propels your startup into the future.

CHAPTER FIFTEEN

BUILDING AI-FIRST HUMAN LED START-UPS

In the modern digital age, especially post-2024, building and leading a high-impact tech team is no longer just about agile development, shipping fast, or cloud infrastructure — it's about integrating intelligence, automation, and adaptability at every layer. The rise of AI, Agentic AI, generative automation, and real-time decision-making systems has changed how tech startups must structure, hire, and lead their engineering and product teams.

This chapter explores how to build and lead an AI-first, automation-native tech team that drives continuous innovation and scalable impact.

15.1 Redefining the Tech Team: AI-Native by Design

The foundation of any impactful tech team in this new era is AI-native thinking. That means approaching product development, workflows, and customer value with an AI-first mindset — not just using AI as an add-on, but as a core design principle.

For instance, a startup building a healthcare platform should not only enable doctors to monitor patients but also use predictive AI to forecast deterioration, recommend interventions, and automate alerts. This goes beyond traditional software into intelligent systems.

To build such systems, teams now must consist of:

- AI/ML Engineers: Experts who can build, fine-tune, and monitor models
- Prompt Engineers: Specialized in interacting with LLMs and designing reusable, structured prompts
- Agent Architects: Who build multi-agent systems that can reason, act, and collaborate (e.g., automating insurance claims end-to-end)
- Data Engineers: Who prepare, clean, and pipeline large datasets efficiently
- Cloud DevOps with MLOps Expertise: For scalable, automated model deployment

Example:

A supply chain optimization startup now uses Agentic AI to simulate multiple demand-supply scenarios autonomously and recommend procurement strategies. The team includes an LLM engineer, a reinforcement learning expert, and an Agent Flow Orchestrator using platforms like LangChain or AutoGPT.

15.2 Tech Culture in the Age of AI: Speed, Ethics, and Autonomy

A high-impact team today must be built on three modern pillars:

- Speed with safety: Rapid iteration is vital, but AI introduces ethical and bias-related risks. Teams need guardrails, testing, and red teaming practices for AI models.

- Ethical innovation: Embed responsible AI practices, privacy-first thinking, and explainability by design. For example, fintechs using credit risk models must avoid racial/gender bias in scoring models.
- Autonomous ownership: With automation taking over repetitive tasks, humans in the loop now focus on decision quality, problem framing, and innovation, not just execution.

15.3 Modern Team Roles & Structures

In an AI-first startup, traditional roles expand or evolve:

- CTO / Chief AI Officer: Drives AI strategy, builds internal capabilities, ensures responsible AI implementation.
- AI Product Manager: Frames problems, defines model success metrics, integrates human feedback into loop design.
- Agentic Workflow Designer: Designs agent pipelines (e.g., retrieval $\rightarrow$ reasoning $\rightarrow$ action) for customer support bots, knowledge workers, etc.
- Automation Engineer: Works with RPA, Zapier, or no-code/low-code stacks to automate business workflows.
- Data & Compliance Officer: Ensures GDPR/DPDP/AI Act compliance, fairness audits, and model observability.

Example:

At a global recruitment startup, the traditional recruiter role is being augmented by an AI agent that screens resumes, ranks candidates, and auto-generates interview questions. The tech team now includes:

- A model trainer using GPT-4 for resume parsing
- An automation lead integrating HR systems
- An AI ethics analyst reviewing decisions monthly

15.4 AI-Native Hiring: Skills + Systems Thinking

In the new world, hiring must go beyond traditional coding tests. You're now looking for people who:

- Understand how to frame problems for LLMs
- Can integrate open-source models and APIs like OpenAI, Claude, or Hugging Face
- Know how to work in prompt loops, vector databases, embeddings
- Think in systems, not features
- Even roles like frontend engineers must now know how to integrate AI assistants, build voice/chat interfaces, or create LLM-driven UX flows.

Interview Example: Instead of asking "reverse a linked list," ask:

"How would you use an LLM to summarize 10,000 support tickets into top 5 insights in less than a minute?"

15.5 Leading with Intelligence: Beyond Traditional Management

Modern tech leadership requires new superpowers:

- AI Literacy for Leaders: You must understand what GPTs can and cannot do, how agents function, and where hallucination risks lie.

- Dynamic Resourcing: You're not just managing people now — you're managing AI + human collaboration.
- Enabling Experimentation: LLMs evolve rapidly. Empower teams to experiment, test new models, and even build custom small language models if needed.

Example:

At an edtech startup, the CTO allocated 10% of engineering time to "AI playgrounds," where engineers explored tools like Ollama, LangChain, and Anthropic's Claude. One such side project evolved into a core feature: an AI mentor for students that boosted retention by 28%.

15.6 Tools for the AI-Driven Team

Tech teams today use tools that mix traditional and intelligent workflows:

- Collaboration: Slack + Notion + AI copilots (Notion AI, Slack GPT)
- Code & Dev: GitHub Copilot, Replit Ghostwriter, VS Code with AI agents
- Data & ML: Weights & Biases, Hugging Face Hub, LangChain, Pinecone, Qdrant
- Automation: Zapier, n8n, Retool, UIPath, AutoGPT
- AI Infrastructure: AWS Sagemaker, Google Vertex AI, Azure OpenAI, NVIDIA Triton Inference Server
- Use auto-documentation, AI-assisted QA, and semantic search to reduce manual toil.

15.7 Remote, Asynchronous, and AI-Augmented Teams

- Remote and hybrid teams are the default — but the next evolution is "agent-augmented" collaboration.

- Use AI agents to summarize Slack threads, generate action items from meetings, and automate ticket grooming.
- Set up AI pair programming buddies for juniors to learn faster.
- Use AI moderators in brainstorming sessions to synthesize inputs and propose ideas.

Example:

A B2B SaaS startup runs Monday meetings with a GPT agent that listens in, summarizes takeaways, and updates Jira. Engineers review this instead of taking manual notes.

15.8 Retaining and Evolving Tech Talent in the AI Age

Retention now depends on growth, relevance, and trust. People want:

- Access to cutting-edge AI tools and learning opportunities
- A role in shaping product strategy, not just shipping features
- Visibility into how AI affects their future role

Strategies:

- Offer AI learning credits or internal AI hackathons
- Involve engineers in product thinking, not just delivery
- Have transparent discussions on AI's impact on jobs, showing how their roles are evolving, not being replaced

15.9 Case Study: Building an AI-Augmented Customer Success Platform

A startup launched a platform that enables SMEs to manage support using AI agents. The core tech team had:

- A CTO who designed multi-agent pipelines
- A designer building LLM-native UX interfaces (context windows, user memory, etc.)
- Backend engineers integrating LangChain + Pinecone
- A prompt engineer writing smart flows for customer resolution bots
- A QA tester using AI to simulate thousands of scenarios
- They shipped the MVP in 6 weeks, and by using agentic support bots, their clients reduced support costs by 40% within 3 months.

Conclusion: AI-First, Human-Led

The nature of high-impact tech teams is evolving. Tomorrow's winning startups will be those who master human-AI collaboration, where machines handle repetitive work, and humans handle creativity, ethics, and strategic insight.

As a founder or leader, your new challenge is not just building an engineering team — it's building a human-AI hybrid team that learns, adapts, and innovates continuously.

Hire for curiosity. Lead with clarity. Embed intelligence everywhere. The future isn't just tech-driven — it's AI-augmented, purpose-led, and automation-powered.

Scaling Sustainably — Building a Profitable, Impactful Business

The excitement of early startup success — a great product, first paying customers, investor interest — often leads to a common trap: scaling too fast, too soon, or without the right foundations. True success lies not in how rapidly you grow, but how sustainably, profitably, and meaningfully you scale.

This chapter explores how to scale a tech startup the smart way: balancing growth with profitability, short-term wins with long-term value, and digital innovation with real-world impact.

16.1 What Is Sustainable Scaling?

Sustainable scaling means growing your business in a way that:

- Maintains financial discipline
- Protects customer experience and product quality
- Preserves your culture and mission
- Builds compounding value — not just top-line vanity metrics

It's the opposite of the "blitzscale at all costs" model that burned through billions in the 2010s. Post-pandemic and post-VC reset, the best founders are those who know how to scale responsibly, not recklessly.

16.2 Profitability Is Cool Again

For years, startups were rewarded for growth over profitability. But as market conditions shift, especially in emerging markets like India, founders are re-discovering a powerful truth:

Profit is not just survival — it is strategic freedom.

When you're profitable:

- You don't depend on investors to survive.
- You can reinvest in innovation, culture, and customer success.
- You have leverage in negotiations (with customers, vendors, and VCs).

? Example:

Zoho, a SaaS company from Chennai, never raised external VC funding and built a billion-dollar business focused on profitability, engineering excellence, and long-term customer value. This allowed it to weather market downturns with ease and retain control over its vision.

16.3 Aligning Growth with Margins

- Scaling doesn't mean just selling more — it means selling smartly.
- Focus on high-margin products or customer segments.
- Use pricing levers: bundle services, introduce tiered pricing, upsell value.
- Replace manual onboarding with automated flows to improve gross margins.

? Example:

A B2B SaaS startup selling CRM tools initially spent ₹ 15,000 onboarding every new client manually. By building an interactive AI onboarding assistant, they cut costs by 80%, improving CAC payback period dramatically without touching the price.

16.4 Don't Hire to Solve Scaling Problems — Solve Them First

A common mistake in scaling: throwing people at problems.

Instead, ask:

- Can this be automated?
- Can this be productized?
- Can AI or bots do this 80% as well?

? Example:

A healthcare tech startup used to have 3 full-time staff managing prescription data entry. They replaced this with an OCR + AI pipeline that read prescriptions, matched to medicine databases, and auto-filled 90% of the data. Instead of hiring 5 more staff, they redirected the team to customer success roles.

16.5 Build Systems Before You Grow

Think of your startup as a rocket. Scaling without systems is like firing boosters without checking the engine.

Before scaling:

- Build dashboards for real-time metrics
- Design knowledge bases for internal documentation
- Create repeatable SOPs for customer onboarding, escalation, and QA
- Set up financial discipline: unit economics, cost controls, monthly P&L tracking

? Example:

An edtech company used Notion to document every key SOP, from teacher onboarding to student support. When they expanded from 3 cities to 20, new teams could be onboarded in a week using these digital playbooks — no chaos, no delays.

16.6 Scaling with Impact: Purpose-Driven Business Models

Sustainable startups are not just profitable — they're purpose-led.

Purpose is not PR. It's the north star that aligns your team, attracts loyal customers, and drives mission-based innovation.

Ask:

- What real-world pain are we solving?
- Who benefits beyond shareholders?
- Can our model create jobs, savings, access, or joy for underserved users?

? Example:

DeHaat, an Indian agritech company, built a profitable model by helping farmers access better seeds, loans, and markets — not just through a flashy app, but by creating a real-world distribution network of agri-entrepreneurs, transforming rural economies sustainably.

16.7 When to Scale? Look for the Signals

Scale when the business pulls you forward, not when you push it ahead forcefully.

Healthy signals you're ready to scale:

- Positive unit economics: CAC < LTV, gross margins stable
- Repeatable sales process with consistent win rate
- Product-market fit (PMF) with low churn and high NPS
- Strong internal systems and team stability
- Demand outpacing capacity

? Example:

A fintech company offering lending-as-a-service waited until it had 3 repeat enterprise clients, a self-serve onboarding platform, and a 4-month CAC payback before doubling its sales team — and saw 3x revenue growth without burning extra capital.

16.8 Scale Through Partners, Not Just Teams

Instead of scaling only through direct hires or capital-heavy expansion, consider:

- Channel partnerships: local resellers, consultants, affiliates
- Franchise models: for industries like healthtech, retail tech, education
- White-label opportunities: let others brand your tech

? Example:

A queue management solution expanded into 100+ hospitals not through direct sales, but by partnering with hospital IT vendors and biomedical suppliers, who bundled the solution with their existing services. This allowed rapid, capital-light growth.

16.9 Financial Discipline: Metrics to Master

Before you scale, you must track and master these numbers:

- LTV / CAC Ratio: At least 3:1
- Gross Margins: Aim for 60%+ (higher in SaaS)
- Net Burn Rate: Keep burn multiples < 1.5x ideally
- Monthly Recurring Revenue (MRR): Track growth % and churn % monthly
- EBITDA Margins: Target profitability or near-breakeven post-PMF

Set a simple Monthly Financial Check-in rhythm with your leadership team. Build this discipline early — it compounds.

16.10 Culture That Scales

A startup's culture can either become a superpower or a silent killer during scaling.

- Codify your values (example: "Speed, with Safety")
- Encourage autonomy with accountability
- Invest in leadership coaching for first-time managers
- Communicate transparently, especially during rapid changes
- Watch for burnout signs, especially post-funding or after hypergrowth sprints

? Example:

A mobility tech company created a 2-hour "Culture Bootcamp" for every new hire, where founders shared stories, values, and what success looked like. This helped preserve their DNA even as they doubled headcount in 6 months.

16.11 Scaling Tech: Don't Let Your Stack Collapse

Your tech must scale with the business. Watch for:

- Monolith codebases that slow down releases
- Hardcoded logic that breaks with new SKUs or users
- Data silos that make reporting painful

Invest early in:

- Microservices or modular architecture
- Cloud scalability (use autoscaling, CDNs)

Observability: logs, metrics, alerts

Don't be the startup that went viral — and crashed during the spike.

16.12 AI & Automation for Scalable Impact

- Use AI and automation to amplify people, not replace them.
- AI chatbots to reduce support load
- Agentic AI to power sales emails, lead scoring, or proposal generation
- Automated reconciliation for finance
- AI tools for internal documentation summarization

? Example:

A SaaS company used ChatGPT fine-tuning to generate custom help center articles from Jira tickets. This reduced ticket volume by 40% and improved CSAT from 3.8 to 4.5 within 2 months — without hiring more support staff.

Conclusion: Grow Wisely, Lead Boldly

Sustainable scaling is the true startup superpower. It's not just about growth, but growth with soul, sense, and systems. Profitability isn't the end of ambition — it's the beginning of resilience.

Build a business that scales without breaking your people, your mission, or your margins. Balance bold bets with operational excellence. Let impact be your multiplier.

Because a startup that scales with purpose doesn't just last — it leads.

Sustainable Scaling Guide: Profitable, Impactful Growth for Startups

To effectively use the checklist version of Chapter 15: Scaling Sustainably — Building a Profitable, Impactful Business, you can guide startup founders or team members to treat it as a self-assessment and action planner. Here's how they should fill it out:

? Instructions for Using the Checklist

- Print or Digitally Track: Use a printed version or a shared digital tool (e.g., Google Sheets, Notion, Trello) to maintain visibility and accountability.
- Review Each Item Carefully: Read each checklist item under the relevant section (Profitability, Impact, Scalability, etc.).

Score Progress:

? Done – This item is already implemented and working well.

? In Progress – Efforts are underway, but it's not fully in place.

? Not Started – This area still needs attention.

Add Notes & Owners:

- For each item, note down who is responsible, the expected timeline, and any dependencies or blockers.
- Include notes on metrics used to track it (e.g., ROI %, CAC/LTV ratio, NPS score).

Review Monthly:

- Set up a recurring review (monthly or quarterly) with your leadership or core team.
- Update status, celebrate completed items, and adjust timelines or tactics as needed.

☑ Sample Checklist Section: Profitability Drivers

Checklist Item	Status (☑/☑/✗)	Owner	Notes / Metrics
CAC < LTV Achieved	☑	Growth Lead	Currently at 1:2, target 1:3
High-margin revenue stream identified	☑	CEO	Enterprise licensing yielding 70% GM
Automated billing & collections in place	✗	Finance Head	Evaluating Stripe vs Razorpay Subscriptions

Sample Checklist - Progess Tracking

Best Practices While Filling It Out

- Be honest and critical — This is a strategic tool, not just a to-do list.
- Involve cross-functional leaders — Product, Sales, Ops, and Tech leads should contribute.
- Customize for context — Feel free to add items specific to your domain or business model (e.g., D2C, SaaS, B2B2C).
- Use it to trigger discussion — It's great for OKR planning, board prep, or investor updates.

Section 1: What Is Sustainable Scaling?

Definition: Scaling your business in a way that balances financial discipline, operational efficiency, product quality, and long-term impact.

Why it matters:

- Avoids premature scaling pitfalls
- Builds compounding customer value
- Preserves team morale and culture

Checklist:

Section 2: Profitability as Strategy

Insight: Profit is strategic freedom, not just survival.

Examples:

- Zoho's bootstrapped billion-dollar success

- Small SaaS firm re-investing profits into R&D

Checklist:

Section 3: Growth With Margins

Tips:

- Focus on high-margin segments
- Bundle, tier, or repackage offers
- Use automation to reduce service costs

Example: B2B SaaS firm automating onboarding with AI to cut costs by 80%

Checklist:

Section 4: Build Before You Scale

Key Pillars:

- Systems
- Documentation
- Automation

Example: Edtech firm using Notion playbooks to expand to 20 cities smoothly

Checklist:

Section 5: Purpose-Driven Scaling

Insight: Purpose attracts talent, loyalty, and capital.

Example: DeHaat empowering agri-entrepreneurs while staying profitable

Checklist:

Section 6: When to Scale

Signals:

- PMF validated
- CAC payback < 12 months
- Product is stable and customers are delighted

Checklist:

Section 7: Scaling Through Partners

Approaches:

- Channel/affiliate models
- Franchising (health, education)
- White-label licensing

Example: Queue management tool expanding via biomedical vendors

Checklist:

Section 8: Financial Discipline Metrics

Core Metrics:

- LTV/CAC > 3
- Gross Margin > 60%
- Monthly burn < 1.5x growth rate
- MRR Growth / Churn Rate
- EBITDA Margins for later-stage

Checklist:

Section 9: Culture and Team Alignment

Principles:

- Communicate values early
- Train first-time managers
- Avoid burnout with pace, not pressure

Example: 2-hour founder-led culture bootcamps

Checklist:

Section 10: Scalable Tech and Automation

Essentials:

- Modular architecture
- Cloud native infra
- Automated QA and testing

Example: Using agentic AI for help center auto-generation

Checklist:

Section 11: Closing Notes

Scale with sense, not just speed. Profit with purpose. Build with systems.

Visual Summary: Available on request as a Notion board / deck.

Let this guide be your north star for building a business that doesn't just grow fast — but grows wisely, profitably, and with lasting impact.

CHAPTER SEVENTEEN

FUTURE HORIZONS — TECH TRENDS THAT WILL SHAPE TOMORROW'S STARTUPS

The startup landscape is entering a transformative era. Emerging technologies — from generalized AI to Web3, spatial computing to automation-as-a-service — are rapidly reshaping how we build, scale, and deliver value. Founders who anticipate these shifts early and embrace them thoughtfully are positioned to lead the next wave of innovation. This chapter unpacks these disruptive forces, illustrating practical ways startups can integrate them to build not just faster, but smarter, fairer, and more impactful companies.

17.1 The Rise of Generalized Artificial Intelligence (AI)

Artificial Intelligence is no longer confined to narrow tasks like image recognition or chatbot replies. We're now witnessing the rise of agentic AI — systems that can reason, plan, and act autonomously across domains. These AI agents are evolving to mimic human-like judgment and task execution, unlocking transformative productivity gains.

Example:

Imagine a startup that builds and sells online courses. Traditionally, you'd need different people for customer support, content QA, lead qualification, and marketing operations. With agentic AI (powered by tools like CrewAI or AutoGen), you can deploy virtual agents to:

- Screen resumes and schedule interviews (HR Agent)
- Qualify leads via email or chat (Sales Agent)
- Run daily code reviews on product releases (DevOps Agent)

These agents can use large language models (LLMs) like Mistral or Phi-3 combined with orchestration layers (LangChain) to interact with APIs, fetch data, take actions, and even hand off tasks to human teammates when necessary.

Actionable Tip: Start experimenting with open-source agents like OpenDevin or create internal "AI interns" using your startup data and workflows.

17.2 Web3 & Decentralization for Trustless Systems

Web3 isn't just about crypto speculation — it's about programmable trust. Startups can use blockchain technology to enable trustless, transparent, and traceable systems, removing the need for centralized intermediaries.

Example:

A freelance platform for designers can use smart contracts on Polygon to automate payments. The contract releases payment automatically once the design is approved. No disputes, no delays.

Other applications include:

- Tokenized loyalty: Reward early users with tradable tokens that appreciate in value as your platform grows (e.g., community contributors on Mirror.xyz).
- Decentralized identity (DID): Verify customer or employee credentials via Ceramic or Verifiable Credentials without exposing sensitive data.
- Use Case: A DAO (Decentralized Autonomous Organization) crowdfunds for a startup and gives contributors voting rights on product features via governance tokens.

Tools to Explore: Chainlink (data oracles), IPFS (decentralized storage), Ceramic (identity), Polygon (blockchain), *Layer one X (L1X - The most advanced Blockchain system in the world today)*

17.3 The Metaverse, Spatial Computing & Digital Twins

Digital experiences are evolving from 2D screens to 3D, immersive environments where people can collaborate, learn, or transact more naturally.

Example:
A SaaS startup launches its product using a virtual showroom on Mozilla Hubs, where investors can walk around, engage with interactive demos, and chat with avatars of the team — all in a spatially aware environment.

- AR/VR Onboarding: Train factory workers using Quest headsets and realistic simulations instead of paper manuals.
- Digital Twins: Use real-time digital replicas of machines or environments to simulate failures, test optimizations, or reduce downtime.
- Startup Application: A logistics startup creates a digital twin of a warehouse to model space utilization and energy consumption, reducing costs by 20%.

Tools to Try: Babylon.js, Spatial.io, Ready Player Me (avatars), Unity, Unreal Engine.

17.4 *Quantum Computing & Edge Intelligence*

Though still in early development, quantum and edge computing are poised to disrupt domains that rely on real-time decision-making and massive data crunching.

Example:
A med-tech startup designing custom cancer drugs can use Quantum AI to simulate molecular structures and optimize treatment combinations, reducing research timelines.

Meanwhile, a smart wearable startup could use Edge AI via Edge Impulse to detect early cardiac anomalies from wristbands without relying on the cloud, ensuring faster response and data privacy.

Action Tip: Stay in the loop with open tools like Qiskit (IBM Quantum), Google Quantum AI, and join Edge AI communities like TinyML.

17.5 Responsible Tech, Ethics, and Digital Well-being

As builders of the future, startups have a moral and strategic duty to embed ethical frameworks into their technologies from day one.

Best Practices:

- Ensure AI transparency and fairness using toolkits like AI Fairness 360 (IBM).
- Design interfaces that promote mindful use, not addiction — for example, limit notification loops or use grayscale themes at night.
- Prepare for regulations like the EU AI Act, India's DPDP Act, or HIPAA for healthcare startups.

Example:

A mental wellness app includes an "AI Therapist" trained on clinically vetted data, but also makes it clear it's not a substitute for professional help, includes opt-outs, and anonymizes all user data.

Toolbox: DPDP compliance sandboxes (India), GDPR frameworks, B Corp Certification pathways.

17.6 Automation-as-a-Service (AaaS)

The next evolution of SaaS is AaaS — not just providing tools, but automating outcomes. These systems use APIs, AI models, and trigger-based workflows to operate like mini virtual employees.

Example:
A growth-stage startup uses Relevance AI to deploy an AI agent as its COO assistant. It:

- Reviews KPI dashboards
- Schedules meetings with underperforming teams
- Suggests next steps using company SOPs
- Sends nudges to update sales forecasts

This blend of AI + APIs + Automation replaces many manual workflows and enhances consistency.

Tools to Test: AgentOps, SuperAgent, LangChain + Zapier + Notion combo setups

17.7 Founder Re-Skilling & Lifelong Learning

In the age of exponential tech, the founder is the bottleneck if learning stagnates. Staying curious and adaptable is your best insurance.

Approach:
Use ChatGPT, Perplexity, and YouTube to run learning sprints on topics like zero-knowledge proofs, GPT agents, or behavioral economics.

- Follow people like Naval Ravikant, Lex Fridman, or Andreessen Horowitz's Future podcast.

- Join hackathons, no-code build weekends, or tech bootcamps like Buildspace or Replit.

Tip: Build 1 mini-tool or app every month — even just for yourself.

17.8 Startup Models of the Future

The line between founder and team is blurring. The future startup might just be:

- 1 Solopreneur + 10 AI agents
- A global collective DAO with revenue-sharing tokens
- A zero-code app launched in 48 hours using tools like Glide, Softr, or Bubble
- A GPT-powered legal co-pilot for SMBs, priced at $20/month with no human staff

These models emphasize speed, scale, and decentralization — but also require a shift in mindset from control to orchestration.

17.9 Preparing for the Unknown

The only constant is change. To future-proof your startup, focus on:

- Building a Tech Radar: Stay updated on breakthroughs (join newsletters like TLDR, Ben's Bites, or Exponential View).
- Human + Tech Fusion: Solve real problems with emerging tools. Don't build "tech for tech's sake."

- Agile Decision-Making: Bake adaptability into your org design, culture, and funding model.
- Think like a technologist (what's possible), a humanist (what's needed), and a strategist (what's viable).

Conclusion: From Awareness to Action

The future is not distant — it's already peeking in. Whether you're building in healthtech, climate, fintech, or creator tools, the emerging stack is yours to leverage. But these tools are only as impactful as the problems they solve.

Let your imagination stretch into the possible — but back it with systems, ethics, and learning.

Your edge isn't just code. It's your courage to imagine, discipline to execute, and wisdom to steward technology responsibly.

CHAPTER EIGHTEEN

MANAGING RAPID INNOVATION

The AI landscape is rapidly evolving, marked by significant advancements in autonomous agents, infrastructure challenges, and societal implications. Here's an overview of the latest developments, organizational challenges, and the road ahead:

? Latest Developments in AI Agents

1. Manus AI: Autonomous Task Execution

Developed by Chinese startup Monica, Manus AI is a fully autonomous agent capable of independently executing complex tasks such as website creation, stock analysis, and travel planning. It operates asynchronously in the cloud, allowing tasks to proceed without constant supervision. Manus has demonstrated strong performance on benchmarks like GAIA, though it faces challenges with system stability and limited public access. Tech

Transformation+9Wikipedia+91950.ai+9

2. DeepSeek-R1: Efficient Reasoning Agent

DeepSeek-R1 is a low-cost reasoning model that has gained attention for its efficiency and adaptability. Developers have utilized techniques like distillation and reinforcement learning with proprietary data to enhance its performance, making it a viable option for businesses seeking cost-effective AI solutions.

3. Genspark: Agentic Search Engine

Genspark offers a team of AI agents that assist users with search, deep research, and various tasks, delivering trustworthy answers and comprehensive results. Its agentic engine represents a shift towards more interactive and intelligent search experiences. Genspark

?? Challenges Faced by Organizations

- Infrastructure Demands: The deployment of advanced AI agents requires significant computational resources, leading to increased costs and the need for specialized hardware.
- Rapid Innovation Pace: The swift development of AI technologies can outpace an organization's ability to integrate and manage them effectively, causing strategic and operational challenges.
- Job Displacement Concerns: The automation capabilities of AI agents raise concerns about potential job losses, particularly in roles involving repetitive tasks.
- Ethical and Privacy Issues: The autonomous nature of AI agents introduces complexities related to accountability, data privacy, and ethical decision-making.

- Security Vulnerabilities: AI agents can be susceptible to cyber threats, necessitating robust security measures to prevent misuse or manipulation.

? The Road Ahead

- Hybrid AI Models: Combining general-purpose AI with specialized agents can offer flexibility and efficiency, catering to diverse organizational needs.
- Open-Source Collaboration: Leveraging open-weight models like Meta's Llama allows for customization and community-driven improvements, fostering innovation.Financial Times
- Regulatory Frameworks: Developing comprehensive regulations will be essential to address ethical, legal, and societal implications of AI deployment.
- Workforce Reskilling: Investing in education and training programs can help the workforce adapt to new roles created by AI advancements.
- Sustainable AI Practices: Focusing on energy-efficient models and infrastructure can mitigate environmental impacts associated with AI technologies.

As AI agents become more integrated into various sectors, organizations must navigate the balance between leveraging technological advancements and addressing the accompanying challenges. Strategic planning, ethical considerations, and continuous learning will be key to harnessing the full potential of AI while mitigating risks.

CHAPTER NINETEEN

THE FOUNDER'S MANIFESTO — A CALL TO ACTION

"The best way to predict the future is to create it." – Peter Drucker

The world is not waiting. Technologies are evolving, societies are shifting, and new challenges are emerging faster than ever. In this volatile, complex, and interconnected world, founders are not just building startups — they're shaping the future of civilization.

This chapter is your call to action. A reminder that the journey you're on is not ordinary. It's extraordinary. And it demands courage, clarity, and commitment.

1. Think Beyond Profit — Build for Purpose

Yes, revenue matters. But legacy matters more.

- Create companies that solve real human problems, not just friction points.

- Ask yourself daily: ***"If my startup disappeared tomorrow, would the world miss it?"***

Examples: A telehealth platform saving rural lives. A carbon tracking SaaS that helps SMEs decarbonize. A mental wellness app restoring self-worth.

? Action: Define your startup's "why" — a reason that transcends quarterly numbers.

2. Be a Founder of the Future, Not the Past

The future belongs to those who adopt exponential tools early and build with them.

- Use AI agents, blockchain, AR/VR, quantum, and automation as your superpowers.
- Don't wait for tech maturity — experiment, prototype, fail fast, learn faster.

? Action: Pick one emerging tech and integrate it into your product, process, or pitch within 30 days.

3. Build Systems, Not Just Startups

- You're not just creating a product. You're creating a movement.
- Design cultures of experimentation, not control.
- Build distributed, AI-augmented teams.
- Replace silos with open APIs and open minds.

?? Action: Map out your startup as a system. What are the inputs, flows, and feedback loops? How can you make it adaptive?

4. Embed Ethics and Empathy in Every Line of Code

- Technology without ethics is dangerous. But technology with empathy is transformative.
- Privacy is not a feature — it's a right.
- Design for inclusion, transparency, and digital well-being.
- Be the founder who says "no" to dark patterns and "yes" to trust.

? Action: Review your product for ethical blind spots using tools like AI Fairness 360 or the Humane Tech checklist.

5. Learn Relentlessly. Evolve Relentlessly.

- The best founders are not know-it-alls. They're learn-it-alls.
- Build your knowledge stack across tech, economics, storytelling, philosophy, and design.
- Schedule learning sprints just like product sprints.
- Make your mind your most compounding asset.

? Action: Set a personal goal to master one new domain every 90 days — and share what you learn with your team.

6. Lead with Conviction, Not Conformity

- The world has enough startups. What it needs is more brave startups.
- Don't build "me-too" products. Build "never-before" visions.
- Dare to say, "This is broken — and I will fix it."

? Action: Write a public Founder's Letter that declares your startup's stand on a global issue — from climate to AI ethics to education.

7. Find Your Tribe — and Lift Others Up

- No founder builds alone. Your network is your runway.
- Engage with global founder communities, forums, hackathons, and idea exchanges.
- Help others rise — especially underrepresented voices in tech and entrepreneurship.

? Action: Mentor one aspiring founder or contribute to an open innovation project this month.

8. Be Ready to Pivot, But Never to Quit

- Markets shift. Tech evolves. What doesn't change is the grit and growth mindset of a true founder.
- Pivot your product, not your purpose.
- Let failure be your greatest feature update.

?? Action: Document your past 3 failures and extract one system/process improvement from each.

Conclusion: You Are the Code of the Future

You are not just a startup founder. You are a technologist, philosopher, systems thinker, and humanist rolled into one.

You are the algorithm that will decide whether humanity stagnates or leaps forward.

And the best part? You don't need permission.

So go — build what matters. Solve what hurts. Create what lasts.

Your Next Steps:

- Revisit your Vision > Value > Velocity framework.
- Re-align your OKRs with next-gen technologies.
- Print this manifesto and read it every time you feel lost, tired, or stuck.
- Share it with one person who needs a spark.

Startup isn't a job. It's a revolution. And you are leading it.

Free Ai & Tech Enablement Tools
For Founders

? No-Code & Website Builders

- Webflow – Design and launch responsive websites visually.
- Carrd – Create simple, responsive one-page sites.
- Dorik – Build beautiful websites without code.
- Super – Turn Notion pages into fast, functional websites.
- Ghost – Publish, share, and grow a business around your content.

? Email Marketing & CRM

- HubSpot CRM – Manage customer relationships and marketing.
- Mailchimp – All-in-one marketing platform for small businesses.
- MailerLite – Create email marketing campaigns with ease.
- ConvertKit – Email marketing for creators.
- EmailOctopus – Affordable email marketing platform.

? Automation & Workflow

- Zapier – Connect your apps and automate workflows.
- Make – Visually create, build, and automate workflows.
- Parabola – Automate data tasks without code.
- Phantombuster – Automate lead generation and data extraction.
- Axiom – Automate browser tasks without coding.

? AI & Content Generation

- ChatGPT – AI-powered conversational agent.
- Copy.ai – AI-powered copywriting tool.
- Writesonic – AI writing assistant for marketing content.
- Jasper – AI content platform for teams.
- Rytr – AI writing assistant for various content types.

? Analytics & Data

- Google Analytics – Track and report website traffic.
- Plausible – Simple and privacy-friendly analytics.
- PostHog – Product analytics suite.
- Matomo – Open-source web analytics platform.
- Hotjar – Understand how users behave on your site.

? Design & Branding

- Canva – Design presentations, social media graphics, and more.

- Figma – Collaborative interface design tool.
- BrandBird – Create branded images for social media.
- Coolors – Generate color palettes.
- FontPair – Pair Google Fonts together.

?? Project Management & Collaboration

- Trello – Visual tool for organizing work and tasks.
- Asana – Manage team projects and tasks.
- Notion – All-in-one workspace for notes, tasks, and databases.
- Slack – Team communication and collaboration.
- ClickUp – Productivity platform for teams.

? Customer Support & Chatbots

- Tidio – Live chat and chatbot solution.
- Landbot – Build conversational chatbots without coding.
- Chatwoot – Open-source customer engagement suite.
- Joonbot – No-code chatbot builder.
- Conferbot – Simple no-code chatbot builder.

? Learning & Resources

- Coursera – Online courses from top institutions.
- edX – Access 2000 free online courses from 140 leading

institutions worldwide.

- Startup School by Y Combinator – Free online program for startup founders.
- Khan Academy – Free online courses, lessons, and practice.
- MIT OpenCourseWare – Free lecture notes, exams, and videos from MIT.

? Hosting & Deployment

- Netlify – Deploy modern web projects.
- Vercel – Frontend hosting platform.
- GitHub Pages – Host websites directly from your GitHub repository.
- Heroku – Cloud platform for deploying apps.
- Render – Cloud hosting for developers.
- For a more extensive list and detailed descriptions, you can explore the following resources:
- Shno's 200+ Free Tools for Startups – A comprehensive, hand-curated list covering various categories.
- Startup Savant's 64 Best Startup Tools – A selection of free or low-cost tools for startups in 2025.
- Startup Geek's 357 Best Startup Tools – An extensive compilation of tools for startup founders.

These tools are designed to help you maximize efficiency, reduce costs, and accelerate growth. If you need assistance selecting tools tailored to your specific startup needs, feel free to ask!

Open-source Ai Agents And Llms Comparison

Open-source AI Agents and LLMs Comparison

Open-source AI agents and Large Language Models (LLMs) are revolutionizing the way we approach artificial intelligence. Here's a comparison of these two technologies:

Key Differences

- AI Agents: AI agents are designed to perform specific tasks, such as data analysis, customer support, or workflow automation. They can be trained on proprietary or open-source models and are often used in enterprise settings.
- LLMs: LLMs are a type of AI model that excels in natural language processing tasks, such as text generation, translation, and summarization. They can be used for various applications, including chatbots, content creation, and language translation.

Open-source LLM Frameworks

Some popular open-source LLM frameworks include :

- AutoGen: Developed by Microsoft Research, AutoGen enables asynchronous conversations among specialized agents. It's well-suited for scenarios requiring real-time concurrency and multiple LLM interactions.
- LangGraph: LangGraph offers explicit control over DAG (Directed Acyclic Graph) workflows, making it ideal for

complex multi-step tasks with branching and advanced error handling.

- Semantic Kernel: This framework focuses on skill-based orchestration and enterprise integrations, providing robust support for multi-language and enterprise compliance.

Comparison of Open-source and Proprietary LLMs

When choosing between open-source and proprietary LLMs, consider the following factors :

- Transparency and Customization: Open-source LLMs offer transparency and customization options, making them suitable for developers who need control over the model.
- Performance and Ease of Use: Proprietary LLMs, such as those from OpenAI and Anthropic, provide state-of-the-art performance and ease of use, making them a practical choice for those who need reliable, high-performing AI models.
- Budget and Resources: Open-source LLMs can be a cost-effective choice for those with limited resources, while proprietary models offer more convenience at a higher cost.

Popular Open-source LLMs

Some notable open-source LLMs include:

- - GPT-Neo
- - GPT-J
- - LLaMA (Large Language Model Meta AI)

By understanding the strengths and weaknesses of open-source AI agents and LLMs, developers can make informed decisions about which technology to use for their specific use case.

Glossary Of Ai, Agent, And Metaverse Terms

? AI & Machine Learning

- LLM (Large Language Model): AI trained on massive datasets that can generate human-like text (e.g., GPT-4, Claude, Mistral).
- NLP (Natural Language Processing): AI's ability to understand and interact in human language.
- Prompt Engineering: Crafting questions or instructions to get desired responses from AI models.
- Fine-tuning: Tailoring a general AI model for specific use cases using additional data.
- RAG (Retrieval-Augmented Generation): Combines live data retrieval with AI generation for more accurate outputs.
- Embeddings: Numerical representations of text used for semantic search and similarity matching.

? AI Agents, Automation & Intelligence Stack

- AI Agent: An autonomous software powered by LLMs that performs a task (e.g., data entry, lead gen).
- Autonomous Agent: An AI that performs actions without constant human intervention using tools, memory, and reasoning.
- Super Agent: An advanced multi-functional AI agent capable of handling complex workflows across domains

(e.g., combining sales, research, coding).

- Multi-Agent System: A group of specialized agents working together to complete a larger task (e.g., CrewAI, AgentVerse).
- CrewAI: A framework that lets you assign agents to specific roles (e.g., researcher, strategist, coder) like a real team.
- LangChain: A developer framework for chaining together LLMs and tools into powerful AI pipelines.
- Memory Store: The ability for agents to retain context and "learn" from past interactions.
- Task Decomposition: Breaking large goals into smaller tasks and assigning to agents.
- Chain of Thought Reasoning: AI's step-by-step reasoning process to solve complex problems.

? Model Context Protocol (MCP)

- MCP (Model Context Protocol): An architecture where multiple LLMs, agents, databases, and tools plug in like modules to form a complete AI ecosystem. Example: An MCP can have a research module (Claude), a writing module (GPT-4), a code module (Code Llama), and a memory module (Vector DB).
- Cognitive Architecture: The design behind how agents, LLMs, tools, and data interact to simulate decision-making.
- Vector Store: A database that stores embeddings for search and memory recall by AI agents (e.g., Pinecone, Weaviate).

? *Metaverse, Virtual Collaboration & 3D Workspaces*

- Metaverse: Persistent 3D virtual environments where people interact using avatars for work, play, or education.
- Virtual Office: A simulated digital workspace with avatars, spatial audio, screensharing, and collaborative tools.
- Spatial Audio: Audio that simulates real-life directionality in virtual spaces.
- Avatar: A digital representation of a user in a virtual environment.
- Immersive Experience: A digital environment engaging multiple senses, often through VR/AR.
- Digital Twin: A virtual replica of a real-world object, space, or person.

?? *No-Code, Tools, and Integration*

- No-code Platform: A tool that allows building software/apps without writing code (e.g., Softr, Bubble).
- Low-code Platform: Requires minimal coding to build applications (e.g., Retool, Appsmith).
- API (Application Programming Interface): Allows software to talk to each other and integrate functionalities.
- Webhooks: Event-based triggers that allow different systems to communicate in real time.

- Automation Framework: A tool that automates workflows and business logic (e.g., Zapier, n8n).
- Prompt Marketplace: A place to buy/sell reusable prompts for AI platforms (e.g., PromptBase).

? Startup-Specific AI Terms

- AI-First Startup: A company that uses AI as its foundational advantage, not an add-on.
- Solopreneur: A single founder running an entire business, often powered by AI and automation.
- AI Stack: The combination of LLMs, agents, frameworks, memory, tools, and APIs that power a founder's business logic.
- Tech Stack: All the tools and technologies used to run your startup (AI + hosting + no-code + payment gateways, etc.).

Your First 90-day Plan With Tech Stack

? Phase 1: Days 1–30 — Validate & Prototype

Goal: Validate your idea, define your audience, and build a simple MVP.

Tasks:

- Define your niche and user persona.
- Validate the idea using AI-powered surveys and Reddit/ forums.
- Build landing page to collect emails.
- Build MVP (no-code or low-code).
- Start early user interviews.

Tech Stack:

- Market Research: ChatGPT, Tally.so, Google Trends
- Landing Page: Carrd, Dorik, Webflow
- MVP Development: Glide, Bubble, Thunkable
- User Interviews: Calendly, Loom, Notion

? Phase 2: Days 31–60 — Build & Launch

Goal: Launch your MVP, get your first users, and iterate fast.

Tasks:

- Launch MVP to early adopters.
- Start building an audience (Twitter, LinkedIn,

IndieHackers).
- Use analytics + feedback to improve.
- Set up simple automations and customer support.
- Prepare email onboarding.

Tech Stack:

- Analytics: PostHog, Plausible
- Email Onboarding: MailerLite, ConvertKit
- Automation: Zapier, Make, Phantombuster
- Live Chat/Support: Tidio, Chatwoot
- Content & Social: Canva, Buffer, Hypefury

? Phase 3: Days 61–90 — Optimize & Scale

Goal: Optimize product, increase visibility, and generate MRR.
   Tasks:

- Launch on Product Hunt, Reddit, LinkedIn.
- Collect and showcase testimonials.
- Run growth experiments (SEO, email, referrals).
- Start charging — even if it's $5/mo.
- Plan next 90 days for scaling.

Tech Stack:

- Product Launch: Product Hunt, Launchpedia
- SEO Tools: Ahrefs Webmaster Tools, Ubersuggest
- Referral/Growth: Rewardful, SparkLoop
- Payment & Billing: LemonSqueezy, Stripe, Gumroad
- Feedback Collection: Senja, Canny

? Output by Day 90:

- MVP live and tested
- First 100 users
- Early revenue (or beta waitlist)
- Repeatable growth channels
- Automated core ops (onboarding, email, support)

Faqs On Topic Addressed In The Book

1. What is the core idea of "AI AGENTERPRISE"?
It's about building high-impact tech startups using AI agents, open-source tools, and minimal resources — without relying on heavy funding.

2. How has startup building changed in the AI era?
Founders now use AI, automation, and global digital tools to validate, build, and scale startups with fewer people and less capital.

3. What does "built by code, not by cash" mean?
It refers to creating scalable businesses using code and AI tools instead of large financial investments.

4. What is the difference between the old and new startup playbook?
Old: Raise funds, hire, build, scale.
New: Use free AI, build MVPs with open source, automate teams, and scale via global tools.

5. Why is now the best time to start a tech company?
Access to free AI, no-code tools, open source, automation, and global talent makes startup building easier and cheaper than ever.

6. What is an MVP?
A Minimum Viable Product — the simplest version of a product used to validate a business idea quickly.

7. What are LLMs and why are they important?
Large Language Models (LLMs) are AI models like GPT or LLaMA that understand and generate human-like text, crucial for automating many tasks.

8. What role does open-source play in startups?
It provides free, customizable code libraries to build products faster without starting from scratch.

9. What is no-code development?

It's building apps or websites using drag-and-drop tools without writing traditional code.

10. How can founders validate an idea using AI?

By prompting AI agents to simulate market research, analyze demand, generate customer personas, and draft business models.

11. Who is the "new-age founder"?

A multi-skilled individual using AI to handle coding, marketing, design, and sales without a large team.

12. What does "AI handles 60% of the load" mean?

AI agents and automation perform repetitive and time-consuming tasks, freeing up the founder's time.

13. What is the mindset shift from scarcity to leverage?

It means using tools, knowledge, and community as multipliers — not waiting for more money or people.

14. What is leverage in a startup context?

It's using existing tools, frameworks, and talent to multiply output with limited input.

15. What are AI agents?

They are intelligent software programs that can perform tasks autonomously — like coding, writing, customer support, etc.

16. What are Super Agents?

Advanced AI agents that can handle multiple complex tasks across domains with higher autonomy.

17. What are MCPs?

What Does MCP Do?

The Model Context Protocol (MCP) is an open standard designed to make large language models (LLMs) more powerful, interactive, and adaptable by enabling them to seamlessly connect with external tools, databases, APIs, and systems.

Traditionally, LLMs like GPT, Claude, or LLaMA work in a static context—they generate responses based only on the prompt and their pre-trained knowledge. MCP changes this by allowing LLMs to dynamically call external functions, fetch real-time data, or trigger workflows during a conversation.

? How It Works:

MCP defines a standardized protocol for communication between an LLM and external components.

Developers register "tools" (like calculators, CRMs, search APIs, or internal services) with metadata and access instructions.

The LLM can then "reason" when to call a tool, send a structured request (via MCP), receive a result, and integrate it into its response—all in real-time.

?? Example Use Case:

Imagine a customer support chatbot using MCP:

A user asks: "What's the status of my order #4789?"

The LLM recognizes the need to fetch live order data.

Through MCP, it queries the company's order management system.

It returns: "Your order #4789 is in transit and will arrive tomorrow."

? Why It Matters:

Modularity: Easily plug in or swap tools and APIs.

Scalability: Build agent ecosystems where each LLM can use hundreds of tools.

Standardization: MCP provides a common language for LLM-tool integration, reducing complexity.

In essence, MCP turns LLMs from static responders into intelligent, tool-using agents—capable of real-world action and personalized utility.

18. How can I build without breaking the bank?
Use free LLMs, open-source tools, startup cloud credits, and AI frameworks to minimize costs.

19. What are startup credits?
Free or discounted access to cloud platforms, tools, and services offered to early-stage startups by companies like AWS, Google, or Microsoft.

20. What are virtual offices?
Digital spaces where remote teams meet, collaborate, and build businesses without physical locations.

21. How can I create my first virtual room?
Use platforms like Gather, Spatial, or FrameVR to set up a 3D or 2D office and invite team members.

22. How do I run a virtual demo or expo?
Host immersive, interactive experiences using VR tools, 3D product walk-throughs, and live AI assistants.

23. What bots can I use in virtual spaces?
Sales bots, onboarding bots, or interactive guides that explain your product or service in real time.

24. What is a solo founder startup?
26. What is CrewAI?
CrewAI is a framework that allows you to manage multiple AI agents working collaboratively toward a common business goal.

27. How do AI agents simulate a startup team?
They replicate functions like coding, writing, design, and customer support — replacing roles like developers, marketers, and analysts.

28. What is an AI funnel?
An automated marketing and sales process using AI to attract, engage, convert, and retain customers with minimal human input.

29. How do feedback loops help in scaling a startup?
They continuously collect user data, improve the product, and guide decision-making — often using AI analytics tools.

30. What are some examples of AI-powered solopreneurs?
Individuals building SaaS tools, e-commerce stores, or digital services using GPT, automation platforms, and self-service infrastructure.

31. How can startups raise funding post-traction?
By demonstrating real users, revenue, and product-market fit — achieved through bootstrapped growth using free tools.

32. What are automation frameworks?
Predefined workflows and tools that replace manual work, like Zapier, Make, n8n, and custom AI pipelines.

33. How do global platforms give access to talent?
Sites like Fiverr, Upwork, and Toptal connect startups with experts across the world at competitive costs.

34. What is meant by "virtual sales"?
Selling products or services via digital channels — using AI chatbots, landing pages, video pitches, and email automation.

35. How does AI help in digital marketing?
It generates content, manages ads, tracks performance, and optimizes campaigns using data-driven insights.

36. What's the advantage of using open-source vs. custom software?
Open-source tools reduce time and cost while allowing flexibility and collaboration from a global developer community.

37. What is an immersive experience in startup demos?
An interactive, often 3D or VR-based product demo that

engages users emotionally and functionally.

38. How can founders learn AI quickly?

Through curated YouTube playlists, prompt engineering guides, community forums, and hands-on use of tools like ChatGPT.

39. What is prompt engineering?

Crafting effective inputs (prompts) to get desired outputs from AI models like ChatGPT or Claude.

40. What is an agent ecosystem?

A setup where multiple AI agents work together — handling tasks like strategy, writing, research, and development.

41. How can I validate a startup idea in 24 hours?

Use GPT to analyze market demand, generate user personas, test messaging, and build a landing page with feedback.

42. What does "build once, deploy globally" mean?

Digital products can be created once and sold worldwide using cloud platforms, AI localization, and online sales.

43. What are community-driven startups?

Companies that grow through active user communities who contribute feedback, code, or promotion.

44. What role does AI play in product design?

AI tools like Uizard, Galileo, and Figma AI help design interfaces, prototypes, and user flows rapidly.

45. How can I automate customer support?

Using AI chatbots like Intercom, Tidio, or GPT-based bots to answer FAQs and handle support tickets.

46. What's the best way to collect user feedback?

Through AI-embedded surveys, heatmaps, behavior tracking, and social listening tools.

47. What is "no-code AI"?

Building intelligent systems using drag-and-drop AI

platforms like Peltarion, Akkio, or Bubble + OpenAI plugins.

48. How do AI agents handle product documentation?

They write, format, and update technical and user documentation based on code or product input.

49. Can AI help in investor outreach?

Yes, by generating investor lists, writing cold emails, pitch decks, and simulating investor Q&A.

50. How do you maintain work-life balance as a founder with AI?

By offloading routine tasks to AI agents and bots, founders can focus on strategy while still getting rest.

51. What are Virtual Co-Founders?

AI agents or tools that take on roles like CTO, CMO, or COO, helping solo founders run startups with the efficiency of a team.

52. How can AI assist in legal and compliance tasks?

AI tools can draft contracts, analyze regulations, generate privacy policies, and monitor for compliance risks.

53. What is a metaverse workspace?

A virtual 3D environment where team members can interact, present, collaborate, and simulate real-world office behavior.

54. How can AI help personalize customer experiences?

By analyzing behavior and preferences, AI tailors messages, product suggestions, and offers to each user.

55. What is an MVP and how do I build one fast?

A Minimum Viable Product is a basic version of your product built using no-code, low-code, or open-source tools to validate the idea.

56. How can I run a startup with zero coding skills?
Use no-code tools, AI app builders, prompt-based workflows, and community support to launch and scale your idea.

57. What is a productized service?
A packaged service offering with fixed scope, price, and delivery process — often automated with AI for scale.

58. What is a digital twin in startups?
A virtual model of a product, process, or system that simulates performance using real-time data and AI.

59. How do bots assist in demos and expos?
Bots can guide visitors, answer FAQs, collect leads, and present product features in real-time during virtual events.

60. What are startup credits and how can I get them?
Free cloud, API, or tool credits offered by companies like AWS, Google, or Notion to early-stage startups via accelerator programs.

61. What is SuperPrompting?
Using layered, multi-step prompts to guide AI through complex reasoning, decision-making, or creative processes.

62. What is the AI Product Stack?
A collection of tools that power AI-based products — including model APIs, prompt platforms, UI/UX layers, and feedback loops.

63. What is a 'Lean AI Startup'?
A startup model focused on minimizing cost and maximizing learning using AI for quick experiments and rapid iteration.

64. What's the role of community in modern startups?
Community brings feedback, referrals, support, and credibility — often reducing marketing and customer acquisition costs.

65. What are MCPs (Multi-Channel Personalities)?

AI personas customized for different platforms (email, WhatsApp, Twitter, etc.) to maintain brand voice and interaction across channels.

66. What are Super Agents?

Highly capable AI agents designed to perform complex, multi-step tasks autonomously with little to no human input.

67. How does AI improve decision-making?

By analyzing vast data, detecting patterns, and simulating outcomes to offer evidence-based insights.

68. What is a command center in AI startups?

A centralized dashboard to track key metrics, AI agent activities, customer data, and growth indicators in real time.

69. What's the benefit of asynchronous work in AI startups?

AI agents work 24/7, allowing continuous progress regardless of human availability or time zones.

70. What is digital-first scaling?

Growing a business entirely through online platforms, tools, and marketing with minimal physical infrastructure.

71. What's a micro-SaaS?

A small, focused software-as-a-service business often run by solo founders solving a niche problem.

72. What is voice interface integration?

Adding voice-based interaction (via Alexa, Google Assistant, or custom voice bots) to improve accessibility and UX.

73. How can I build a personal brand with AI?

Use AI to generate thought leadership content, schedule social media posts, and engage with your audience automatically.

74. What's the role of avatars in virtual startups?
Avatars represent team members or AI agents in metaverse offices, demos, or virtual onboarding experiences.

75. What is prompt chaining?
Connecting multiple prompts in a sequence to complete complex workflows, like turning a user idea into a business plan.

76. What is the use of AI in customer support?
AI-powered chatbots and virtual assistants handle FAQs, troubleshoot issues, and provide instant responses 24/7, improving customer satisfaction and reducing support costs.

77. What is an immersive pitch room?
A virtual or metaverse-based environment where founders can showcase their product, vision, and traction using interactive visuals, bots, and 3D storytelling.

78. How can AI help in onboarding customers?
Through personalized walkthroughs, dynamic FAQs, and automated training modules tailored to each user's behavior and needs.

79. What's the benefit of async learning with AI?
Learners access personalized content at their own pace, with AI adapting lessons based on performance and interest.

80. How do digital assets increase startup valuation?
Proprietary datasets, trained AI models, and digital IPs offer long-term defensibility and value, attracting investors.

81. What is frictionless design in AI startups?
Creating interfaces and workflows that are intuitive, require minimal input, and reduce user drop-off — often with AI assistance.

82. How do you build a content engine with AI?
Use tools like ChatGPT, Jasper, or Copy.ai to generate blogs,

posts, emails, and scripts on autopilot, fed by user or market data.

83. What is the AI x Automation flywheel?

A feedback loop where AI analyzes results of automation, improves the process, and triggers better outcomes with each cycle.

84. How do solopreneurs scale using AI?

By using AI for marketing, customer support, design, development, and analytics — freeing them to focus on strategy and sales.

85. What are low-latency workflows?

Systems and processes that respond quickly and seamlessly to inputs, often using AI to minimize lag and delays in user experience.

86. How do you test an idea before building it?

Use AI to generate landing pages, run ads, collect feedback, and validate demand without building the full product.

87. What is a zero-code prototype?

An early version of a product built entirely using drag-and-drop or prompt-based platforms without any programming.

88. What is swarm intelligence in AI agents?

A model where multiple AI agents collaborate like a hive mind, learning from each other and distributing tasks efficiently.

89. What is AI-powered fundraising?

Using AI to generate pitch decks, identify investor matches, schedule outreach, and simulate valuation scenarios.

90. What is a plug-and-play SaaS?

A software solution that can be quickly set up and used with minimal onboarding, often with pre-configured templates or AI suggestions.

91. How can AI improve hiring decisions?
By analyzing resumes, scoring candidates, predicting culture fit, and even conducting video interviews with emotion and tone analysis.

92. What's the difference between a chatbot and an AI agent?
Chatbots follow scripts; AI agents reason, learn, adapt, and make decisions, functioning more like team members.

93. What are the risks of relying on AI?
Bias in data, over-automation, hallucinations, lack of emotional intelligence, and security risks if not properly managed.

94. How can I protect my startup idea while using AI?
Avoid sharing sensitive info with public models; use private deployments, NDAs, and IP frameworks to protect innovation.

95. What is the AI-native mindset?
Designing businesses, workflows, and teams assuming AI is a core member — not just a support tool.

96. What's the significance of agent memory?
It allows AI agents to recall past tasks, user preferences, or project history — enabling continuity and personalization.

97. How can AI speed up market research?
By scanning competitors, analyzing trends, summarizing customer reviews, and identifying gaps in seconds.

98. What is conversational UI?
Interfaces where users interact with software through natural language, often powered by chatbots or voice assistants.

99. What's the future of solopreneurship with AI?
Empowered by AI agents, solopreneurs will build high-impact startups without traditional teams, infrastructure, or investment.

100. What's the next big shift after AI-first startups?
Agent-native enterprises — startups run by coordinated networks of AI agents with minimal human oversight, maximizing speed, scale, and sustainability.